# IN THE WORDS OF
# RONALD REAGAN

# In the
# Words of
# Ronald Reagan

## The Wit, Wisdom, and Eternal Optimism
## of America's 40th President

### Compiled by Michael Reagan

### with Jim Denney

## Nelson Books
**A Division of Thomas Nelson Publishers**
*Since 1798*

www.thomasnelson.com

Published in Nashville, Tennessee, by Thomas Nelson, Inc.

Unless otherwise noted, all photos courtesy of the Ronald Reagan Library.

Originally published under the title *The Common Sense of an Uncommon Man* (Thomas Nelson, 1998)


ISBN 0-7852-7023-X


*Printed in the United States of America.*

04 05 06 07 08  QW  9 8 7 6 5 4 3 2

# CONTENTS

# CONTENTS

The Reagan family on the campaign trail in 1980
Me and my son, Cameron, Dad, Nancy, Patti, and Ron Jr.

# *F*OREWORD

## The Value of His Words

I vividly remember Day One of the Reagan Era.

It began on Tuesday, January 20, 1981—Ronald Reagan's inauguration as the fortieth president of the United States. The Reagan family began that morning with an early service at St. John's Episcopal Church, "the church of the presidents," where we gathered to pray and give thanks.

Later we went to the Capitol building for the swearing-in ceremony. It was Dad's idea that the president be sworn in on the west side of the Capitol for the first time in history. That site afforded the crowd a magnificent view—the majestic spire of the Washington Memorial, the marble-domed rotunda of the Jefferson Memorial, the stately colonnade of the Lincoln Memorial mirrored in the reflecting pool, and across the Potomac, the hallowed ground of Arlington.

My wife, Colleen, and I stood on the banner-draped platform along with Dad and Nancy and the rest of the Reagan family. Also on the platform were the speaker of the House, the justices of the Supreme Court, and various political leaders. Before us was a crowd of a hundred thousand people. I was choked up and misty-eyed as Dad placed his hand on his mother's worn, cracked, Scotch-taped Bible and took the oath of office as prescribed by the Constitution he reveres so deeply. Then, continuing a tradition begun by George Washington, Dad gave a comparatively brief but stirring inaugural address. With a wave of his hand, he gestured toward the monuments that gleamed in the brilliant January sunshine. "Standing here," he said, "one faces a magnificent vista opening up on this city's special beauty and history. At the end of this open mall are those shrines to the giants on whose shoulders we stand." With those great words, he called a nation to remember its great history and to look ahead to its shining future.

Afterward Colleen and I attended a luncheon in the Statuary Hall of the Capitol, ringed about by statues representing every state in the Union. Members of the House and Senate, Supreme Court justices, friends, and family were there. At the beginning of the luncheon, Dad received the news, which he immediately passed on to those in the hall: After 444 days in captivity, the fifty-two Americans held hostage in Iran had been released and were on their way home via Germany. "I couldn't ask for a better Inaugural Day gift than that, " Dad concluded. The hall erupted in spontaneous applause. Dad later offered former president Jimmy Carter one last trip aboard Air Force One, to go to Germany and meet the hostages.

There were many other events that day—a parade, a reception in the Red Room of the White House, a Reagan family photo session, and more. It was sobering to notice that, as Dad went about his ceremonial duties that day, he was always accompanied by a military attaché carrying the black briefcase with nuclear launch codes. It was strange to think the strong but loving hands that had held mine when I was a child now had a finger on the Doomsday Button.

There were nine inaugural balls around the city that night, and Dad and Nancy put in an appearance at each of them. Colleen and I hosted the gathering at the Washington Hilton Hotel, the first stop for the new president and his first lady. Before going to greet the crowd, Dad, Nancy, Colleen, and I gathered in a holding room. There Dad—looking elegant and dapper in white tie and tails—checked his hair in the mirror. Then he whirled about, jumped up in the air, and clicked his heels—not a bad feat for a fellow just a few weeks shy of seventy!

"I'm the president of the United States!" he announced with a wink.

We all laughed. "Yes, Dad, " I said, "you sure are!"

Then we all went out to greet the other celebrants in the ballroom.

A few weeks after the inauguration, I received a letter from Dad, in which he had enclosed a second one, addressed to Cameron, our toddler. In the letter to me, Dad mentioned that a letter he had written to a friend shortly after the inauguration had already been sold to a collector for $10,000. So Dad suggested that if Cameron ever wanted to sell the enclosed letter, my son could probably use the proceeds for his college education.

In his handwritten letter to Cameron, Dad said there was one woman still in Iran who had not been released with the other hostages on Inauguration Day and that he was in the midst of negotiations for her release. "The secretary of state is now coming to my office to tell me whether the offer the United States has made to Iran is accepted," Dad wrote (as it turned out, she was released soon afterward). The letter was signed, "Love, Grandpa. P.S. Your grandpa's name is Ronald Reagan, the president of the United States."

Cameron still has that letter, and I can tell you one thing for sure: Those words from his grandpa are worth a lot more to our family than $10,000. They are literally priceless.

The longer I live, and the more deeply I delve into the actions, words, and thoughts of Ronald Reagan, the more I treasure them. I am in awe of this great man. I am in awe of his accomplishments: the restoration of the American economy, the American military, and the American spirit—not to mention the collapse of the iron curtain. Inauguration Day 1981 was a watershed in American history. Looking back on the new American revolution that began that January day, he reflected at the end of his presidency, "Once you begin a great movement, there's no telling where it will end. We meant to change a nation, and instead we changed a world."

As you delve into the wit and commonsense wisdom of this uncommon man, I think you will be as impressed with the value of his words as I am. Encouraged by my editor, Janet Thoma, and assisted by my associate, Jim Denney, I've explored the archives of the Ronald Reagan Presidential Library as well as my own memories to produce this collection of what I believe are the best and most enduring of my father's reflections on a wide range of subjects.

I've also included many personal stories that will give you a richer sense of who Ronald Reagan was—not just the expanse of his thoughts but the depths of his heart. These are the stories and ideas of an American original—and they are truly priceless. So sit back, enjoy, and revel in these pages. I think you are in for a treat.

MICHAEL REAGAN
Sherman Oaks, California

Dad in his acting days in the 1950s with the General Electric Theater

# ACTING

*Without question, Dad's acting career prepared him well for politics—but not in the way you might think. The acting profession didn't just teach him how to carry himself on a stage or play to the camera. It prepared him for the presidency in much more subtle ways. Good actors learn early that their craft is not just a game of let's pretend.*

*I've been in actors' workshops, and I've even done a bit of acting on television—just enough to develop a deep respect for the stage and screen accomplishments of my parents, and enough to know that my place is on radio! A lot of people think acting is about faking it; that it's a bag of tricks used to present an illusion to the camera. People think that acting is nothing more than being able to emote on cue. Wrong, all wrong. Acting—a genuine dramatic or comedic performance—is about finding the truth within, about summoning and revealing thoughts, feelings, attitudes, and convictions with utter genuineness.*

*Both of my parents saw acting as a process of revealing truth, not creating illusions. My mother, Jane Wyman, would stay in character for days during filming, because that was how she preserved the truth and integrity of her character. Dad rarely had to stay in character, because the roles he played were usually variations on the real Ronald Reagan. He always believed the camera was merciless in detecting insincerity and evasion.*

*The acting profession also prepared my father for the bad reviews and harsh criticism that are part and parcel of public life. He never complained about the relentless attacks against him and Nancy throughout his years in office. By the time he got to the White House, Ronald Reagan had a very thick skin regarding the many unfair and downright stupid things that were written and said in the press.*

*Dad was a good actor. In fact, if he had gotten the kind of roles he truly wanted, I think he might have been a great actor. If you doubt me, take another look at his supporting role as George "the Gipper" Gipp in* Knute Rockne, All American *(1940). Or check out his performance as Drake McHugh in* King's Row *(1942), in which he gave a brilliant one-take performance capped by the unforgettable line, "Where's the rest of me?!"*

*For the most part, Dad was typecast as the romantic lead in lightweight pictures. They were not bad pictures. In fact, they were quite entertaining and successful—mostly comedies such as* John Loves Mary, The Hasty Heart, *and of course,* Bedtime for Bonzo. *He resigned himself to the fact that he had become (as he put it) "the Errol Flynn of the B movies"—an assessment that prompted Errol Flynn himself to say, "I thought I was the Errol*

*Flynn of B movies!" Perhaps if Dad had gotten the roles he really wanted, he never would have gone into politics.*

*There's an interesting story about the filming of* King's Row. *Dad's co-star in the picture was Bob Cummings. Dad and Bob—two very likable, genuinely nice guys—really hit it off and became good friends. Several times on the set of the movie, Bob made a comment that now seems prophetic: "Someday I'm going to vote for this fella for president."*

*Here are some of Dad's thoughts—both funny and serious—about the profession he enjoyed so much during the first half of his life.*

Someone told my old boss Jack Warner that I'd announced for governor. And Jack thought about it for just a second, and then he said, "No, Jimmy Stewart for governor, Ronald Reagan for best friend."

*Campaign rally for Vice President George Bush*
*San Diego, California, November 7, 1988*

Some of my critics over the years have said that I became president because I was an actor who knew how to give a good speech. I suppose that's not too far wrong. Because an actor knows two important things—to be honest in what he's doing and to be in touch with the audience. That's not bad advice for a politician either. My actor's instinct simply told me to speak the truth as I saw it and felt it.

*Conversation with speechwriter Landon Parvin, 1988*

*During his early, lean years as an actor, Dad once received a telegram from his agent, Bill Meilkjohn, which read: WARNER BROS OFFER CONTRACT SEVEN YEARS, ONE YEAR OPTIONS, STARTING AT $200 A WEEK. WHAT SHALL I DO? Dad's immediate reply:*

SIGN BEFORE THEY CHANGE THEIR MINDS.

I saw *Knute Rockne, All-American* on the late show the other night, and it was so hacked up, my 80-yard run was a 5-yard loss.

*Said on various occasions*

In the business that I used to be in, you learn not to stay on stage too long. You learn there's a time you have to exit.

*Evansville, Indiana*
*September 24, 1978*

Dad as George "The Gipper" Gipp in the 1937 movie *Knute Rockne, All American*

# $A$GE

*The "age issue" was a big worry in Dad's 1980 presidential campaign. His sixty-ninth birthday came right at the beginning of the primary season. The campaign staff worried that voters would think him too old to be president. I suggested to Lorelei Kinder, one of Dad's California staffers, that they shouldn't hide his age—they should celebrate it! "If I were you, I'd throw a humongous 'Happy Birthday, Ronald Reagan' party. Rent a big hall, bake a big cake, invite lots of guests, and tie it to fund-raising events nationwide with closed-circuit TV. That way the press can't say he's too old because he's celebrating his age!"*

*Lorelei was dubious at first, but a few weeks later the Reagan campaign rented the Shrine Auditorium, closed-circuited the party around the country, and Ronald Reagan's sixty-ninth birthday party became one of the biggest fund-raisers ever. From then on, neither the press nor Dad's political opponents could get any traction with the age issue.*

*Dad never ran from this issue—he used humor to disarm it.*

# AGE

I will not make age an issue of this campaign. I am not going to exploit, for political purposes, my opponent's youth and inexperience.

*Reagan–Mondale debate*
*Kansas City, Missouri, 1984*

Last year you helped me celebrate the thirty-first anniversary of my thirty-ninth birthday. I don't mind getting older, because I recall that Moses was fifty when God commissioned him for public service, and he lived to be a hundred and twenty. And Abraham was a hundred and his wife, Sarah, ninety when they did something truly amazing! And he lived to be a hundred seventy-five. Just imagine if he had put two-thousand dollars a year into his IRA account!

*Annual National Prayer Breakfast*
*Washington, D.C., February 4, 1982*

If I'm ever in need of any transplants, I've got parts they don't make anymore.

*Washington, D.C.*
*February 10, 1986*

# ALZHEIMER'S DISEASE

*My father walked through the valley of the shadow of an illness called Alzheimer's disease. The world was stunned the day his handwritten letter was publicly released, announcing that he had joined the four million other Americans with this as-yet incurable neurological disease. Especially hard-hit by this news was my daughter, Ashley, who was then eleven years old. Like so many others across the country, she listened to the media reports about her grandpa's illness. She heard one doctor explain what Alzheimer's is and how it makes people forgetful. Then she came into the kitchen, where her mother, Colleen, and I were standing, and she said, "Mom and Dad, I'm going to love Grandpa even if he doesn't know who I am."*

*Here is the text of the two-page letter Dad wrote in his own hand to the American people.*

★

My Fellow Americans,

I have recently been told that I am one of the millions of Americans who will be afflicted with Alzheimer's disease.

8

Upon learning this news, Nancy and I had to decide whether as private citizens we would keep this a private matter or whether we would make this news known in a public way.

In the past, Nancy suffered from breast cancer and I had my cancer surgeries. We found through our open disclosures we were able to raise public awareness. We were happy that as a result many more people underwent testing. They were treated in early stages and able to return to normal, healthy lives.

So now, we feel it is important to share it with you. In opening our hearts, we hope this might promote greater awareness of this condition. Perhaps it will encourage a clearer understanding of the individuals and families who are affected by it.

At the moment I feel just fine. I intend to live the remainder of the years God gives me on this earth doing the things I have always done. I will continue to share life's journey with my beloved Nancy and my family. I plan to enjoy the great outdoors and stay in touch with my friends and supporters.

Unfortunately, as Alzheimer's disease progresses, the family often bears a heavy burden. I only wish there was some way I could spare Nancy from this painful experience. When the time comes I am confident that, with your help, she will face it with faith and courage.

In closing, let me thank you, the American people, for giving me the great honor of allowing me to serve as your President. When the Lord calls me home, whenever that may be, I will leave with the greatest love for this country of ours and eternal optimism for its future.

I now begin the journey that will lead me into the sunset of my life. I know that for America there will always be a bright dawn ahead.

Thank you, my friends. May God always bless you.

Sincerely,

Ronald Reagan

*Saturday, November 5, 1994*

# AMERICA

*Dad's love for America was genuine and boundless. Though he was ever optimistic about America's future, he has always cautioned that America must maintain her reliance upon God and her commitment to righteousness and morality. He was fond of quoting Alexis de Tocqueville's perceptive assessment of the source of America's greatness: "Not until I went into the churches of America and heard her pulpits flame with righteousness did I understand the secret and genius of her power. America is great because she is good, and if America ever ceases to be good, America will cease to be great."*

*Tocqueville's words ring as true today as when they were first conveyed. And so do Ronald Reagan's.*

There is, in America, a greatness and a tremendous heritage of idealism, which is a reservoir of strength and goodness. It is ours if we will but tap it. And because of this—because that greatness is there—there is need in America today for a reaffirmation of that goodness and a re-formation of our greatness.

*Conservative Political Action Conference,*
*Washington, D.C., March 20, 1981*

In America, our origins matter less than our destination, and that is what democracy is all about.

*Republican National Convention*
*Houston, Texas, August 17, 1992*

I believe this blessed land was set apart in a very special way, a country created by men and women who came here not in search of gold but in search of God. They would be free people, living under the law, with faith in their Maker and their future.

*Annual National Prayer Breakfast*
*Washington, D.C., February 4, 1982*

America is the moral force that defeated communism and all those who would put the human soul itself into bondage.

*Republican National Convention*
*Houston, Texas, August 17, 1992*

★

Dad in his second year in office in 1982

I've always believed that this land was placed here between the two great oceans by some divine plan. That it was placed here to be found by a special kind of people—people who had a special love for freedom and who had the courage to uproot themselves and leave hearth and homeland, and come to what, in the beginning, was the most undeveloped wilderness possible. We came from a hundred different corners of the earth. We spoke a multitude of tongues.

We landed on this eastern shore and then went out over the mountains and the prairies and the deserts and the far western mountains to the Pacific, building cities and towns and farms and schools and churches. If wind, water, or fire destroyed them, we built them again. And in so doing, at the same time, we built a new breed of humanity called an American—a proud, independent, and most compassionate individual, for the most part.

Two hundred years ago, Tom Paine—when the thirteen tiny colonies were trying to become a nation—said, "We have it in our power to begin the world over again." Today we're confronted with the horrendous problems that we've discussed here tonight. And some people in high positions of leadership tell us that the answer is to retreat. That the best is over. That we must cut back. That we must share in an ever-increasing scarcity . . .

Well, we, the living Americans, have gone through four wars. We've gone through a Great Depression in our lifetime that was literally worldwide and almost brought us to our knees.

But we came through all of those things, and we achieved even new heights and new greatness. The living Americans today have fought harder, paid a higher price for freedom, and done more to advance the dignity of man than any people who ever lived on this earth.

For two hundred years, we've lived in the future, believing that tomorrow would be better than today and today would be better than yesterday. I still believe that. I'm not running for the presidency because I believe that I can solve the problems we've discussed tonight. I believe the people of this country can. And together we can begin the world over again. We can meet our destiny—and that destiny is to build a land here that will be, for all mankind, a shining city on a hill. I think we ought to get at it.

*The Reagan–Carter debate*
*October 28, 1980*

In this springtime of hope, some lights seem eternal; America's is.

*Acceptance speech, Republican National Convention*
*Dallas, Texas, August 23, 1984*

Don't let anyone tell you that America's best days are behind her—that the American spirit has been vanquished. We've seen it triumph too often in our lives to stop believing in it now.

*Second inaugural address*
*January 21, 1985*

America's best days are yet to come. And I know it may drive my opponents up the wall, but I'm going to say it anyway: you ain't seen nothin' yet.

*Acceptance speech, Republican National Convention*
*Dallas, Texas, August 23, 1984*

Some may try and tell us that this is the end of an era. But what they overlook is that in America, every day is a new beginning, and every sunset is merely the latest milestone on a voyage that never ends. For this is the land that has never become but is always in the act of becoming. Emerson was right: America is the Land of Tomorrow.

*Presidential Medal of Freedom ceremony*
*The White House, January 13, 1993*

From our forefathers to our modern-day immigrants, we've come from every corner of the earth, from every race and every ethnic background, and we've become a new breed in the world.

We're Americans and we have a rendezvous with destiny . . . No people who have ever lived on this earth have fought harder, paid a higher price for freedom, or done more to advance the dignity of man than the living Americans—the Americans living in this land today. There isn't any problem we can't solve if government will give us the facts. Tell us what needs to be done. Then, get out of the way and let us have at it.

*"To Restore America," televised speech during*
*the primary campaign against Republican*
*incumbent Gerald Ford, March 31, 1976*

America represents something universal in the human spirit. I received a letter not long ago from a man who said, "You can go to Japan to live, but you cannot become Japanese. You can go to France to live and not become a Frenchman. You can go to live in Germany or Turkey, and you won't become a German or a Turk." But then he added, "Anybody from any corner of the world can come to America to live and become an American."

*Campaign rally for Vice President George Bush*
*San Diego, California, November 7, 1988*

# THE ASSASSINATION ATTEMPT

*On March 30, 1981—just a few weeks into my father's presidency—he was wounded by a would-be assassin's bullet on a street in Washington, D.C. That bullet lodged about a quarter of an inch from his heart. Even today, few Americans realize how close we came to losing Ronald Reagan. And I can't help wondering how the world would have been changed if that bullet had penetrated a quarter-inch farther. Would America's economy and worldwide prestige have been revived? Would the evil empire of Soviet Communism have collapsed? Would American pride and optimism have been restored? Very doubtful.*

*When Ronald Reagan survived the attempt on his life, he broke a "curse" on the presidency. For more than a century before his election, there had been a seemingly coincidental but rhythmic twenty-year "death cycle" among American presidents. Beginning with William Henry Harrison in 1840, every president elected or reelected in a year ending in zero had died in office. Following Harrison, there was Abraham Lincoln (elected 1860), James A. Garfield (elected 1880), William McKinley (elected 1900), Warren*

*G. Harding (elected 1920), Franklin D. Roosevelt (reelected 1940), and John F. Kennedy (elected 1960). Ronald Reagan's name came within a quarter of an inch of being added to that list.*

Dad waves to the crowd outside the Washington Hilton moments before shots were fired on March 30, 1981. In the ensuing chaos, Dad is thrust into his limo while Secret Service agents and police tackle the gunman and try to assess the situation.

*It was a miracle that Dad survived the assassination attempt—a miracle for the Reagan family and for America. He brought himself and the nation through this crisis with his characteristic humility and good humor.*

*To Nancy on the day of the shooting:* Honey, I forgot to duck.

*March 30, 1981*

*The day after the shooting, Dad was curious about the gunman's motive:* Does anybody know what that guy's beef was?

*March 31, 1981*

*To White House aide Michael Deaver:* I really screwed up the schedule.

*March 31, 1981*

*Dad was shot while wearing a brand-new blue pinstripe suit. It ended up in shreds on the floor of the hospital emergency room. His advice to me, the day after the shooting:* Michael, if you're ever shot, make sure you're not wearing a new suit.

*March 31, 1981*

*Dad was very concerned about the three other men also shot that day, saying in typical show-biz style:* I didn't want a supporting cast.

*March 31, 1981*

*Kidding an attractive nurse:* Does Nancy know about us?

*April 1, 1981*

*When White House aide Lyn Nofziger told Dad, "You'll be happy to know that the government is running normally while you're in the hospital," Dad instantly quipped:* What makes you think I'd be happy about that?

*April 2, 1981*

*After he was told the other three wounded men were improving (Secret Service agent Timothy J. McCarthy, D.C. police officer Thomas Delahanty, and severely injured White House press secretary Jim Brady), Dad said:* That's great news, especially about Jim. We'll have to get four bedpans and have a reunion.

*April 4, 1981*

*When White House aides gathered at his hospital bedside to brief him, he deadpanned:* I knew it would be too much to hope that we could skip a staff meeting.

*April 12, 1981*

*And six years later he said:* Since I came to the White House, I've gotten two hearing aids, had a colon operation, a prostate operation, skin cancer, and I've been shot. Funny thing is, I never felt better.

*March 28, 1987*

# *T*HE BERLIN WALL

Dad, an ex-president now, hammering away at the Berlin Wall in 1990, a wall he helped weaken during his two terms.

*Early in his presidency Dad demonstrated his commitment to ending communism and bringing down the Berlin Wall. In a speech before the British Parliament in 1982, he predicted the end of communism and urged the world to prepare for the post-Communist era.*

From here I will go to Bonn and then Berlin, where there stands a grim symbol of power untamed. The Berlin Wall, that dreadful gray gash across the city, is in its third decade. It is the fitting signature of the regime that built it.

*Address to the British Parliament*
*Palace of Westminster, June 8, 1982*

*My friend Dana Rohrabacher, who is now a congressman from the Forty-fifth District in California, was a White House speechwriter at the time Dad decided to go to Berlin in 1987. Dana told me that my father called his speechwriters together and told them he wanted to give a speech while there in which he would call for the dismantling of the Berlin Wall. So a draft was written, Dad inked in his changes, additions, and finishing touches, and—as is usual with a major foreign policy address—the speech was passed around to all the administration's foreign policy experts.*

*That's when the fertilizer hit the fan. The diplomatic corps went ballistic. The secretary of state went ballistic. The national security adviser went ballistic. "You can't say that, Mr. President!" they remonstrated. "You can't tell Mr. Gorbachev to tear down the wall! He'll be insulted! He'll get mad! We have to stay on his good side!"*

*"Well," said Ronald Reagan, "that wall is an insult to the civilized world. I think it's time we got mad and Mr. Gorbachev tried*

*to get on our good side."*

*Right up until the day before he gave the speech, Dad's own national security adviser begged him not to say anything about tearing down the wall. He even handed Dad an edited draft of the speech and said, "Here, Mr. President, use this version." Dad just smiled and said, "Thanks, but I like the draft I have just fine." Then he went to Berlin and, standing before that ugly gray gash across the face of humanity, sounded a call that reverberated around the world and shook the crumbling foundations of the Soviet Union.*

*Dana Rohrabacher tells me that, just a few days after that speech, the CIA reported that Gorbachev was meeting with his advisers on how to begin dismantling the Berlin Wall as a gesture of peace and goodwill. As president of the United States, Ronald Reagan possessed an inner moral compass that was more certain and accurate than the advice from the brightest minds at State and the NSA. It was his moral conviction, his clear sense of right and wrong that—more than any other factor in history—brought about the end of the Soviet empire and the end of the cold war.*

*Today a large piece of the Berlin Wall—colorfully decorated with butterflies and flowers to symbolize freedom and peace—is on display at the Reagan Presidential Library in Simi Valley, California.*

There is one sign the Soviets can make that would be unmistakable, that would advance dramatically the cause of freedom and peace. General Secretary Gorbachev, if you seek peace, if you seek prosperity for the Soviet Union and Eastern Europe, if you seek liberalization, come here to this gate!

Mr. Gorbachev, open this gate! Mr. Gorbachev, tear down this wall!

*Speech before the Brandenburg Gate*
*West Berlin, June 12, 1987*

It's been years since I stood at the Brandenburg Gate and called for the Wall to come down. It wasn't merely a polite suggestion. I was angry, because as I looked over the Wall into East Germany, I could see the people being kept away. Their government didn't want them to hear what we were saying. But I think that they knew what we were saying, and they wanted a better life.

*Ceremony marking the presentation of*
*a section of the Berlin Wall at*
*the Ronald Reagan Presidential Library*
*Simi Valley, California, April 12, 1990*

# *B*UREAUCRACY AND BUREAUCRATS

If a bureaucrat had been writing the Ten Commandments, a simple rock slab would not have been near enough room. Those simple rules would have read: "Thou shalt not, unless you feel strongly to the contrary, or for the following stated exceptions, see paragraphs 1 through 10, subsection A."

*June 6, 1974*

Bureaucrats favor cutting red tape—lengthwise.

*November 1975*

You don't fix bad policies by rearranging or replacing one bureaucrat with another. You have to replace bad ideas with good ones.

*"Government and the Family: The Need to Restore Basic Values"*
*Televised address to the nation, July 6, 1976*

I just wanted to speak to you about something from the Internal Revenue Code. It is the last sentence of section 509A of the code and it reads: "For purposes of paragraph 3, an organization described in paragraph 2 shall be deemed to include an organization described in section 501C-4, 5, or 6, which would be described in paragraph 2 if it were an organization described in section 501C-3." And that's just one sentence out of those fifty-seven feet of books.

*Address before the Dothan-Houston County Chamber of Commerce*
*Dothan, Alabama, July 10, 1986*

Every once in a while, somebody has to get the bureaucracy by the neck and shake it loose and say, "Stop doing what you're doing!"

*To a Russian student during a question and answer*
*session at Moscow State University, May 31, 1988*

I'm afraid that I have to confess to you that one of the sins of government—and one with which we must deal and never be able to be completely successful with, and this includes our own government—is that the bureaucracy, once created, has one fundamental rule above all others: Preserve the bureaucracy.

*Press conference following the U.S.–Soviet Summit*
*Moscow, June 1, 1988*

You can't be for big government, big taxes, and big bureaucracy and still be for the little guy.

*Campaign rally for Vice President George Bush*
*San Diego, California, November 7, 1988*

Dad speaks at Moscow State University in 1988

Dad in 1984
Just an average citizen

# CITIZEN POLITICIAN

*To think of Ronald Reagan as a politician is not only to underestimate him—it is to completely miss the point. He didn't choose politics. Politics chose him.*

*I know his critics just don't buy it, but it's really true: Ronald Reagan never saw himself as a politician. He was a genuine Washington outsider, just an average citizen who knew something was very wrong with his government—and wanted to set it right. And that's exactly what he did.*

*The Founding Fathers originally envisioned an American government comprised entirely of citizen politicians. Instead of the professional political class that rules America today, they foresaw scores of grassroots Americans serving a term or two in Congress or the White House, then going back home to the farm, the shop, the schoolhouse, the law office, the real world.*

*Ronald Reagan fulfilled that original vision. He saw a job that needed doing, and he volunteered to do it. He got it done—then he went back home and picked up the life he had set aside when he first ran for governor of California—the life of Ronald Reagan, citizen. Here are some of his reflections on his sixteen years in public office.*

I'm just a citizen temporarily in public service.

*As governor of California, 1970*

I'm not a politician by profession. I am a citizen who decided I had to be personally involved in order to stand up for my own values and beliefs. My candidacy is based on my record, and for that matter, my entire life.

*"Government and the Family: The Need to Restore Basic Values"*
*Televised address to the nation, July 6, 1976*

I was happy with my career in the entertainment world, but I ultimately went into politics because I wanted to protect something precious . . . I went into politics in part to put up my hand and say, "Stop." I was a citizen politician, and it seemed the right thing for a citizen to do.

*Farewell address, The Oval Office*
*January 11, 1989*

# THE CITY ON A HILL

*Throughout his political life, Ronald Reagan spoke of his vision for America as a shining city on a hill—an image he borrowed from John Winthrop (1588–1649), the godly Puritan who served as the first governor of the Massachusetts colony. The City on a Hill is a beautiful and inspiring metaphor for America—not as it is but as it could be. It is an expression of an ideal that affirms not only individual freedom but individual responsibility. It is an ideal that does not attempt to solve human problems by taxing, spending, and transferring wealth but by preserving a precious heritage of freedom, moral values, and spirituality. The dream of the shining city is still alive and still achievable—if we work together.*

★

On the deck of the tiny *Arabella* off the coast of Massachusetts in 1630, John Winthrop gathered the little band of pilgrims together and spoke of the life they would have in that land they had never seen: "We shall be as a City upon a Hill. The eyes of all people are upon us, so that if we shall deal falsely with our God in this work we have undertaken and so cause Him to withdraw his present help from us, we shall be made a story and a byword through all the world."

*Eisenhower College fund-raiser speech*
*October 14, 1969*

The past few days when I've been at that window upstairs, I've thought a bit of the "shining City upon a Hill." The phrase comes from John Winthrop, who wrote it to describe the America he imagined. What he imagined was important because he was an early pilgrim, an early freedom man. He journeyed here on what today we'd call a little wooden boat; and like the other pilgrims, he was looking for a home that would be free. I've spoken of the shining City all my political life, but I don't know if I ever quite communicated what I saw when I said it. But in my mind it was a tall, proud city built on rocks stronger than oceans, windswept, God-blessed, and teeming with people of all kinds living in harmony and peace; a city with free ports that hummed with commerce and creativity. And if there had to be city walls, the walls had doors and the doors were open to anyone with the will and the heart to get here. That's how I saw it, and see it still.

And how stands the City on this winter night? More prosperous, more secure, and happier than it was eight years ago. But more than that: After two hundred years, two centuries, she still stands strong and true on the granite ridge, and her glow has held steady no matter what storm. And she's still a beacon, still a magnet for all who must have freedom, for all the pilgrims from all the lost places who are hurtling through the darkness toward home.

We've done our part. And as I walk off into the city streets, a final word to the men and women of the Reagan Revolution, the men and women across America who for eight years did the work that brought America back. My friends: We did it. We weren't just marking time. We made a difference. We made the City stronger, we made the City freer, and we left her in good hands. All in all, not bad, not bad at all.

*Farewell address, The Oval Office*
*January 11, 1989*

# COMMUNISM

Dad and Mikhail Gorbachev at the 1985 Geneva Summit

*Dad detested communism with the same intensity with which he loved freedom—and for the same reason. Communism is the antithesis of freedom. It is collectivist and totalitarian—as opposed to freedom, which allows individuals to reach their maximum potential in an atmosphere of maximum opportunity.*

*As far back as 1981, when everyone was resigned to the seem-*

*ing permanence of communism, Ronald Reagan predicted it would end up on the ash heap of history. He was widely ridiculed for that prediction.*

*But then, prophets usually are.*

The years ahead will be great ones for our country, for the cause of freedom and the spread of civilization. The West will not contain communism, it will transcend communism. We will not bother to denounce it. We'll dismiss it as a sad, bizarre chapter in human history whose last pages are even now being written.

*Notre Dame University*
*May 17, 1981*

The Marxist vision of man without God must eventually be seen as an empty and a false faith—the second oldest in the world—first proclaimed in the Garden of Eden with whispered words of temptation: "Ye shall be as gods."

*Conservative Political Action Conference*
*Washington, D.C., March 20, 1981*

I've come to be a collector of jokes that the Russian people tell among themselves that reveal their feeling about their government. One has to do with when Brezhnev first became president.

He invited his elderly mother to come up and see his suite of offices in the Kremlin and then put her in his limousine and drove her to his fabulous apartment in Moscow. And in both places, not a word. She looked but said nothing. Then he put her in his helicopter and took her out to the country home outside Moscow in a forest. And again, not a word. Finally, he put her in his private jet and took her down to the shores of the Black Sea to see that marble palace which is known as his beach home. And finally she spoke. She said, "Leonid, what if the Communists find out?"

*Eureka College alumni dinner*
*Peoria, Illinois, May 9, 1982*

★

I have one question for those rulers: If communism is the wave of the future, why do you still need walls to keep people in and armies of secret police to keep them quiet?

*July 19, 1983*

★

How do you tell a Communist? Well, it's someone who reads Marx and Lenin. And how do you tell an anti-Communist? It's someone who understands Marx and Lenin.

*Arlington, Virginia*
*September 25, 1987*

# CONGRESS

*Campaigning against the Democratic incumbent, Ronald Reagan promised to improve relations with Congress—even if it was in the hands of the opposition party. This one-liner he used on the campaign stump expresses that commitment:*

Pennsylvania Avenue must be a two-way street.

*Washington, D.C.*
*September 15, 1980*

If the Congress wants to bring the Panamanian economy to its knees, why doesn't it just go down there and run it?

*White House Correspondents Dinner*
*Washington, D.C., April 21, 1988*

Consider for a moment the people you'll be sending to Washington tomorrow. Congress and the president are equal branches of government. When you vote for the Senate or for your local congressional seat, you're voting for the direction of the country and the world as much as when you vote for president. And since we have to ride two horses, Congress and the president, across every stream, shouldn't they both be going in the same direction?

*Campaign rally for Vice President George Bush*
*San Diego, California, November 7, 1988*

# CONSERVATIVES

★

*If you look up the word conservative in the dictionary, you'll find Ronald Reagan's picture there. He defined conservatism in America at the end of the twentieth century. And here, in his own words, is how he defined it:*

★

You know, as I do, that most commentators make a distinction between what they call "social conservatism" and "economic conservatism." The so-called social issues—law and order, abortion, busing, quota systems—are usually associated with the blue-collar, ethnic, and religious groups who are traditionally associated with the Democratic party. The economic issues— inflation, deficit spending, and big government—are usually associated with Republican party members and independents who concentrate their attention on economic matters.

Now I am willing to accept this view of two major kinds of conservatism or, better still, two different conservative constituencies. But at the same time let me say that the old lines that once clearly divided these two kinds of conservatism are disappearing.

In fact, the time has come to see if it is possible to present a program of action based on political principle that can attract those interested in the so-called social issues and those interested in economic issues. In short, isn't it possible to combine the two major segments of contemporary American conservatism into one politically effective whole?

I believe the answer is yes. It is possible to create a political entity that will reflect the views of the great, hitherto conservative, majority. We went a long way toward doing it in California. We can do it in America. This is not a dream, a wistful hope. It is and has been a reality. I have seen the conservative future and it works!

> *"Reshaping the American Political Landscape"*
> *American Conservative Union Banquet*
> *Washington, D.C., February 6, 1977*

Conservatism is the antithesis of the kind of ideological fanatacism that has brought so much horror and destruction to the world. The common sense and common decency of ordinary men and women, working out their own lives in their own way—this is the heart of American conservatism today. Conservative wisdom and principles are derived from willingness to learn—not just from what is going on now, but from what has happened before.

*"Reshaping the American Political Landscape"*
*American Conservative Union Banquet*
*Washington, D.C., February 6, 1977*

This great turn from left to right was not just a case of the pendulum swinging—first, the left holds sway and then the right, and here comes the left again. The truth is, conservative thought is no longer over here on the right; it's the mainstream now. And the tide of history is moving irresistibly in our direction.

*Conservative Political Action Conference*
*Washington, D.C., March 1, 1985*

Perhaps the greatest triumph of modern conservatism has been to stop allowing the left to put the average American on the moral defensive. By average American I mean the good, decent, rambunctious, and creative people who raise the families, go to church, and help out when the local library holds a fund-raiser; people who have a stake in the community because they are the community.

*Conservative Political Action Conference*
*Washington, D.C., March 1, 1985*

Fellow citizens, fellow conservatives, our time is now. Our moment has arrived. We stand together shoulder to shoulder in the thickest of the fight. If we carry the day and turn the tide, we can hope that as long as men speak of freedom and those who have protected it, they will remember us, and they will say, "Here were the brave and here their place of honor."

*Conservative Political Action Conference*
*Washington, D.C., March 20, 1981*

Because ours is a consistent philosophy of government, we can be very clear: We do not have a separate social agenda, a separate economic agenda, and a separate foreign agenda. We have one agenda. Just as surely as we seek to put our financial house in order and rebuild our nation's defenses, so too we seek to protect the unborn, to end the manipulation of schoolchildren by utopian planners, and permit the acknowledgment of a Supreme Being in our classrooms just as we allow such acknowledgments in other public institutions.

*Conservative Political Action Conference*
*Washington, D.C., March 20, 1981*

Sure you are still outnumbered. We're outnumbered in California, three to two. But you know sometimes that makes life a little more simple. When you're outnumbered and surrounded and someone yells "charge," you don't have to ask which direction. Any way you're facing, you'll find a target.

*"Why the Conservative Movement Is Growing"*
*Southern GOP Convention*
*Atlanta, Georgia, December 7, 1973*

Conservatives were brought up to hate deficits and justifiably so. We've long thought there are two things in Washington that are unbalanced—the budget and the liberals.

*Conservative Political Action Conference*
*Washington, D.C., March 1, 1985*

*Dad was a fiscal conservative from Day One. In 1967, when he became governor of California, he discovered that the outgoing administration of Governor Edmund G. "Pat" Brown had left behind reams and reams of official stationery. Dad hated to see all that paper go to waste, so he asked his secretary:*

Couldn't we just X out his name?

# *T*HE CONSTITUTION

The Declaration of Independence and the Constitution of these United States are covenants we have made not only with ourselves but with all mankind. Our founding documents proclaim to the world that freedom is not the sole prerogative of a chosen few. It is the universal right of all God's children.

*Captive Nations Week Conference*
*Los Angeles, California, July 15, 1991*

You know, Senator Kennedy was at a dinner just recently, the ninetieth birthday party for former governor and ambassador Averell Harriman. Teddy Kennedy said that Averell's age was only half as old as Ronald Reagan's ideas. And you know, he's absolutely right. The Constitution is almost two hundred years old, and that's where I get my ideas.

*November 13, 1981*

Two Soviets . . . were talking to each other. And one of them asked, "What's the difference between the Soviet Constitution and the United States Constitution?" And the other one said, "That's easy. The Soviet Constitution guarantees freedom of speech and freedom of gathering. The American Constitution guarantees freedom after speech and freedom after gathering."

*New Britain, Connecticut, July 8, 1987*

I had a copy of the Soviet Constitution and I read it with great interest. And I saw all kinds of terms in there that sound just exactly like our own: "Freedom of assembly" and "freedom of speech" and so forth. Of course, they don't allow them to have those things, but they're in there in the constitution. But I began to wonder about the other constitutions—everyone has one—and our own, and why so much emphasis on ours. And then I found out, and the answer was very simple—that's why you don't notice it at first. But it is so great that it tells the entire difference. All those other constitutions are documents that say, "We, the government, allow the people the following rights," and our Constitution says "We, the People, allow the government the following privileges and rights."

We give our permission to government to do the things that it does. And that's the whole story of the difference—why we're unique in the world and why no matter what our troubles may be, we're going to overcome.

*Address to the United States Senate Youth Program, February 5, 1981*

# CRIME

We no longer walk in the countryside or on our city streets after dark without fear. The jungle seems to be closing in on this little plot we've been trying to civilize for six thousand years.

*Eisenhower College fund-raiser speech*
*October 14, 1969*

Why does a criminal defendant with a clever lawyer seem able to run circles around some of our finest prosecutors with a seemingly bottomless barrel of time-consuming tricks? The public is frustrated and fed up with the sort of behavior that some defendants—and, indeed, some of their lawyers—are seemingly able to get away with in courtrooms, behavior that would not be tolerated in any kindergarten.

*Speech to the California State Bar Association*
*Los Angeles, California, September 20, 1970*

The crime problem has indeed become a matter of widespread concern, even among people of different philosophies. Today's hard-liner on law and order is yesterday's liberal who was mugged last night.

*California, August 1, 1973*

I don't think that making it difficult for law-abiding citizens to obtain guns will lower the crime rate—not when the criminals will always find a way to get them.

*"To Restore America," televised speech during
the primary campaign against Republican
incumbent Gerald Ford, March 31, 1976*

# DEFENSE

Dad inspects the sailors at the recomissioning of the USS *New Jersey* in 1982.

*Following its bitter humiliation in Vietnam, America retreated militarily while the Soviet Union advanced. Soviet military might was projected in Asia, in Nicaragua and Cuba, in the Middle East, in Iraq, and across Africa. Then, in December 1979—while America stood by, wringing its hands—the Soviets brazenly* invaded Afghanistan, a step toward capturing the strategic Persian Gulf region and the rich oilfields of the Arabian peninsula. The United States simply could not afford another four years of aimless defense policy.

In January 1981 Ronald Reagan took charge and immediately reversed America's military decline. He talked tough with the Soviets, calling the USSR what it was—the Evil Empire. And he set the machinery in motion to topple that empire. He rebuilt our faltering military and unveiled the Strategic Defense Initiative, a bold new technological concept that promised to render nuclear missiles obsolete.

The president's tough talk and tough actions reversed a decade of U.S. military decline. His support for freedom fighters touched off a firestorm of liberation, from Nicaragua and Grenada to Eastern Europe and Afghanistan. The Evil Empire collapsed, a victory Ronald Reagan achieved without committing America to war.

If there had been no Ronald Reagan, no military buildup, no Evil Empire speech, no SDI—would the Soviet Union have fallen? Or would America have fallen?

I wonder . . .

We will always remember. We will always be proud. We will always be prepared, so we may always be free.

*Memorial address at Pointe du Hoc, Normandy, France*
*The fortieth anniversary of D day, June 6, 1984*

Our status as a free society and world power is not based on brute strength. When we've taken up arms, it has been for the defense of freedom for ourselves and for other peaceful nations who needed our help. But now, faced with the development of weapons with immense destructive power, we've no choice but to maintain ready defense forces that are second to none. Yes, the cost is high, but the price of neglect would be infinitely higher.

*Recommissioning of the USS* New Jersey
*Long Beach, California, December 28, 1982*

The most fundamental paradox is that, if we're never to use force, we must be prepared to use it and to use it successfully. We Americans don't want war, and we don't start fights. We don't maintain a strong military force to conquer or coerce others. The purpose of our military is simple and straightforward: We want to prevent war by deterring others from the aggression that causes war. If our efforts are successful, we will have peace and never be forced into battle. There will never be a need to fire a single shot. That's the paradox of deterrence.

*"Armed Forces Day," radio address to the nation*
*The White House, May 21, 1983*

None of the four wars in my lifetime came about because we were too strong. It is weakness that invites adventurous adversaries to make mistaken judgments. America is the most peaceful, least warlike nation in modern history. We are not the cause of all the ills of the world. We're a patient and generous people. But for the sake of our freedom and that of others, we cannot permit our reserve to be confused with a lack of resolve.

*Acceptance speech, Republican National Convention*
*Dallas, Texas, August 23, 1984*

There are some who've forgotten why we have a military. It's not to promote war. It's to be prepared for peace. There's a sign over the entrance to Fairchild Air Force Base in Washington state, and that sign says it all: "Peace is our profession."

*Acceptance speech, Republican National Convention*
*Dallas, Texas, August 23, 1984*

There was a time when we depended on coastal forts and artillery batteries because with the weaponry of that day, any attack would have had to come by sea. Well this is a different world, and our defenses must be based on recognition and awareness of the weaponry possessed by other nations in the nuclear age.

We can't afford to believe that we will never be threatened. There have been two world wars in my lifetime. We didn't start them and, indeed, did everything we could to avoid being drawn into them. But we were ill-prepared for both. Had we been better prepared, peace might have been preserved.

*Address to the nation on defense and national security*
*March 23, 1983*

Despite the spread of democracy and capitalism, human nature has not changed. It is still an unpredictable mixture of good and evil. Our enemies may be irrational, even outright insane, driven by nationalism, religion, ethnicity, or ideology. They do not fear the United States for its diplomatic skills or the number of automobiles and software programs it produces. They respect only the firepower of our tanks, planes, and helicopter gunships.

*Commencement address*
*The Citadel, May 15, 1993*

History teaches that wars begin when governments believe the price of aggression is cheap.

*Televised address to the nation*
*January 16, 1984*

# DEMOCRACY

This democracy of ours, which sometimes we've treated so lightly, is more than ever a comfortable cloak, so let us not tear it asunder, for no man knows, once it is destroyed, where or when he will find its protective warmth again.

*Commencement address*
*Eureka College, June 7, 1957*

The great rediscovery of the 1980s has been that, lo and behold, the moral way of government is the practical way of government: Democracy, the profoundly good, is also the profoundly productive.

*Farewell address, The Oval Office*
*January 11, 1989*

The other day, someone told me the difference between a democracy and a "people's democracy" [communism]. It's the same as the difference between a jacket and a straitjacket.

*Human Rights Day speech*
*Washington, D.C., December 10, 1986*

★

The only cure for what ails democracy is more democracy.

*"Democracy's Next Battle"*
*Oxford Union Society*
*Oxford, England, December 4, 1992*

# DEMOCRATIC PARTY

*Ronald Reagan seems to epitomize all that is good and great about the Republican party. So a lot of people are surprised to find out that he was once an FDR Democrat. In fact, during much of the 1950s, he actively campaigned for Democratic candidates and causes. In time, however, he realized that while he was giving speeches about the decline of America, he was supporting and voting for the very people who were contributing to that decline. Finally, he woke up and realized that while he hadn't left the Democratic party, the Democratic party had left him. In fact, it had taken a sharp left turn, away from the values and principles that made America great.*

*One day in 1962 he was giving a speech near his home in Pacific Palisades. Right in the middle of delivering it, a woman jumped up and said, "Mr. Reagan, I have a question. Have you registered as a Republican yet?"*

*"Well, no," Dad admitted, "but I intend to."*

*The woman walked right up the aisle, slapped a voter registration form on his lectern, and said, "I'm a registrar. Sign here." So*

*Dad signed and became a Republican right on the spot.*
  *Then he continued with his speech.*

I have spent most of my life as a Democrat. I recently have seen fit to follow another course. I believe that the issues confronting us cross party lines.

*"A Time for Choosing" (a.k.a. "The Speech")*
*Televised address to the nation on behalf of*
*Barry Goldwater, October 27, 1964*

Millions of Democrats must be made to see that philosophically they have more in common with us than with those who would erode our defenses, pawning our weapons to pay for some new experiment in social reform. And make no mistake about it, there's been no change in the Democratic leadership since that convention of 1972. They are the same people who rediscover poverty every election and promise to cure it. They've cured it so often that they've now made a profession of it. They thrive on failures, on righting wrongs, aiding victims, and so forth. It must be understood that success in those tasks would put them out of business. No matter how many programs are set up and operating, their proponents never claim success for them. To do so would be to say the problems have been solved, meaning the programs are no longer needed. And the programs, not the problems, are their very reason for being.

*"Why the Conservative Movement Is Growing"*
*Southern GOP Convention*
*Atlanta, Georgia, December 7, 1973*

The difference between them and us is that we want to check government spending, and they want to spend government checks.

*Sacramento, California, 1969*

My whole family were Democrats. As a matter of fact, I had an uncle who won a medal once for never having missed voting in an election for fifteen years . . . and he'd been dead for fourteen.

*August 9, 1973*

We've heard a great deal about Republican "fat cats," and how the Republicans are the party of big contributions. I've never been able to understand why a Republican contributor is a "fat cat" and a Democratic contributor of the same amount of money is a "public-spirited philanthropist."

*Speech at a Republican fund-raiser,*
*Los Angeles, California, August 4, 1974*

I know what it's like to pull the Republican lever for the first time, because I used to be a Democrat myself, and I can tell you it only hurts for a minute and then it feels just great.

*Bayonne, New Jersey*
*October 25, 1980*

You know, we could say [the Democrats] spend money like drunken sailors, but that would be unfair to drunken sailors. It would be unfair, because the sailors are spending their own money.

*Acceptance speech, Republican National Convention*
*Dallas, Texas, August 23, 1984*

Over and over they told us they are not the party they were. They kept telling us with straight faces that they're for family values, they're for a strong America, they're for less intrusive government.

And they call me an actor.

*Republican National Convention*
*Houston, Texas, August 17, 1992*

I used to say to some of those Democrats who chair every committee in the House: "You need to balance the government's
checkbook the same way you balance your own." Then I
learned how they ran the House bank, and I realized that was
exactly what they had been doing!

*Republican National Convention*
*Houston, Texas, August 17, 1992*

# DREAMS

Dad is sworn as the fortieth president of the United States in 1981.

*The day of his inauguration as the fortieth president of the United States, Dad raised his right hand, placed his left hand upon the well-worn, well-marked Bible of his late mother, and took the oath of office as prescribed by the Constitution. The Bible was open, and his hand rested on the words God spoke to King Solomon in 2 Chronicles 7:14:*

*If My people who are called by My name will humble themselves, and pray and seek My face, and turn from their wicked ways, then I will hear from heaven, and will forgive their sin and heal their land.*

In the margin next to that verse, his mother Nelle had written, "A most wonderful verse for the healing of the nations." America was in need of healing on that wintry day in January 1981. The nation badly needed to be healed—morally, spiritually, economically, and militarily.

After he had finished taking the oath of office, Dad turned and kissed Nancy. Then the cold air was split by the deafening crack of a twenty-one gun salute. Dad shook hands with other dignitaries on the platform, beginning with outgoing president Jimmy Carter. He turned and ascended to the podium to begin his first inauguration address—and as he began to speak, something magical occurred. Here is how Time *magazine described that moment:*

As he raised his head to look out at the crowd, a strange and wonderful thing happened. The dark cloudy sky over his head began to part slightly, within seconds there was a gaping hole in the gray overcast, and a brilliant, golden shaft of wintry sun burst through the clouds and bathed the inaugural stand and the watching crowd. As Reagan spoke, a slight breeze ruffled his hair and the warm golden light beamed down on him.

*Later, a few minutes after he finished speaking, as if on cue from some master lighter backstage, the hole in the clouds shrank, the sky darkened, and Washington grew gray and cold once again.*

*Quoted by Nancy Reagan in* My Turn
*(New York: Random House, 1989), pp. 233–234*

*You see? Magic! Among the magical words Dad spoke that day was this inspiring, optimistic statement, calling an entire nation to redream together the American dream.*

We are too great a nation to limit ourselves to small dreams. We are not, as some would have us believe, doomed to an inevitable decline. I do not believe in a fate that will fall on us no matter what we do. I do believe in a fate that will fall on us if we do nothing. So, with all the creative energy at our command, let us begin an era of national renewal. Let us renew our determination, our courage, and our strength. And let us renew our faith and our hope. We have every right to dream heroic dreams.

*First inaugural address, January 20, 1981*

We need true tax reform that will at least make a start toward restoring for our children the American dream that wealth is denied to no one, that each individual has the right to fly as high as his strength and ability will take him.

*"A Time for Choosing" (a.k.a. "The Speech")*
*Televised address to the nation on behalf of*
*Barry Goldwater, October 27, 1964*

And what of America's promise of hope and opportunity, that with hard work even the poorest among us can gain the security and happiness that is the due of all Americans? You can't put a price tag on the American dream. That dream is the heart and soul of America. It's the promise that keeps our nation forever good and generous, a model and hope to the world.

*Signing the Tax Reform Act of 1986*
*White House South Lawn*
*October 22, 1986*

# *E*CONOMICS AND ECONOMISTS

Recession is when your neighbor loses his job. Depression is when you lose yours. And recovery is when Jimmy Carter loses his.

*Campaign stump speech, 1980*

A friend of mine was asked to a costume ball a short time ago. He slapped some egg on his face and went as a liberal economist.

*Talk before the President's Commission on White House Fellowships*
*The White House, February 11, 1988*

You know, I told my senior staff in this room the other day that one definition of an economist is someone who sees something happen in practice and wonders if it would work in theory. That's one I can tell; my degree was in economics.

*Talk to business leaders at a briefing on budget reform*
*The White House, March 13, 1987*

# *E*DUCATION

*Because of his great love for education and his hope and optimism for future generations of students, Ronald Reagan was particularly troubled over the violent campus rebellions of the late '60s. "While I was governor," he recalled in* Speaking My Mind, *"the chancellor at UCLA once canceled the playing of the national anthem at commencement exercises because it might be provocative. I know, I was there . . . I was burned in effigy so regularly I must have helped gasoline sales."*

*Despite the loud and angry excesses of the '60s, Dad never lost faith in the young people on our university campuses. On one occasion he addressed a crowd in a university gymnasium in the Midwest. There were about 15,000 people in attendance—two-thirds of them students. During the question-and-answer session after the speech, one older man stood and asked Ronald Reagan about campus rebellion. "Aren't these kids just rebelling against the principles and standards we were raised on and which we've been trying to pass on to them?"*

*"Perhaps today's young people aren't rebelling against our standards," Dad replied. "Perhaps they are rebelling because they don't*

*think we are living by the standards we've tried to teach them."*

*The gym was silent for several moments—then the 10,000 young people in that building jumped to their feet and roared their approval. Finally, someone from the "over-thirty" generation had articulated what these students were feeling.*

It wasn't so very long ago that all I had to do to start an unfriendly campus riot was show up. And now on campaign stop after campaign stop, in state after state, I've seen so many young Americans, like yourselves, coming out to say hello.

*Republican campaign rally*
*Mount Clements, Michigan, November 5, 1988*

Education is like a diamond with many facets: It includes the basic mastery of numbers and letters that give us access to the treasury of human knowledge, accumulated and refined through the ages. It includes technical and vocational training, as well as instruction in science, higher mathematics, and humane letters. But no true education can leave out the moral and spiritual dimensions of human life and human striving. Only education that addresses this dimension can lead to that blend of compassion, humility, and understanding that is summed up in one word: *wisdom.*

*Education Day USA proclamation, April 19, 1986*

St. Thomas Aquinas warned teachers they must never dig a ditch in front of a student that they failed to fill in. To raise doubts and to ever seek and never find is to be in opposition to education and progress. To discuss freely all sides of all questions without values is to ensure the creation of a generation of uninformed and talkative minds. Our obligation is to help our young people find truth and purpose, to find identity and goals.

*Eisenhower College fund-raiser speech*
*October 14, 1969*

In America we created at the local level and administered at the local level for many years the greatest public school system in the world. Now through something called federal aid to education, we have something called federal interference, and education has been the loser. Quality has declined as federal intervention has increased . . . Control of education should be returned to local school districts.

*"To Restore America," televised speech*
*during the primary campaign against Republican*
*incumbent Gerald Ford, March 31, 1976*

Yours is a sacred mission. In the words of Henry Adams, "A

teacher affects eternity." Each of you, as tiring and routine as your daily duties may sometimes seem, is a keeper of the American dream, the American future. By informing and exercising young minds, by transmitting learning and values, you are the vital link between all that is most precious in our national heritage and our children and grandchildren, who will some day take up the burdens of guiding the greatest, freest society on Earth.

*Annual convention of the*
*American Federation of Teachers*
*Los Angeles, California, July 5, 1983*

I remember one day I was sitting in the principal's office. I wasn't invited there for a social visit. And he said something that fortunately stuck in my mind, and I remembered. He said, "Reagan, I don't care what you think of me now. I'm only concerned with what you'll think of me fifteen years from now." And I thank the Lord that I had the opportunity to tell him shortly before he died how I felt about him fifty years after that visit in his office. And he was a very great influence in my life.

*Remarks at the release of a Department*
*of Education report on improving education May 20, 1987*

Secretary [William] Bennett makes, I think, an interesting analogy. He says that if you serve a child a rotten hamburger in America, federal, state, and local agencies will investigate you, summon you, close you down, or whatever. But if you provide a child with a rotten education, nothing happens, except that you are liable to be given more money to do it with. Well, we've discovered that money alone isn't the answer.

*Speech before the National Governors' Association*
*February 22, 1988*

The Reagan family circa 1915
Jack, Neil, Dad, and Nelle

# $F$AITH

*Dad's early spiritual foundation shaped his life, his worldview, and even his political beliefs. When he was a child, schools taught the truth about how our nation began and about the principles of faith America was founded upon. So there was no contradiction between Ronald Reagan's inner life of faith and his view of America's heritage as "one nation under God."*

*Ronald Reagan received a strong grounding in Christian virtues and daily fellowship with God from his devout mother, Nelle—as he describes in this excerpt from his autobiography,* An American Life.

Nelle assumed responsibility for the spiritual preparation of my brother and me. She first took us to Sunday school, then, when we were older, to the main services, but always said she'd leave it up to us to decide whether we wanted to actually join the church. At twelve, I made my decision and was baptized as a member of the Disciples of Christ . . .

I have always prayed a lot; in those days [the Great Depression], I prayed things would get better for our country, for our family, and for Dixon [Dad's hometown in Illinois]. I even prayed before football games . . . I didn't pray to win—I didn't expect God to take sides—but I prayed no one would be injured, we'd all do our best and have no regrets no matter how the game came out.

But I was afraid to reveal this to my older and more sophisticated teammates. Then, to my amazement, everyone in the room said that they prayed—and to my surprise, they all said they prayed along the same lines that I did.

That was the last time I was ever reluctant to admit I prayed.

An American Life

*(New York: Simon & Schuster, 1990), pp. 32, 56*

*Although my father always believed in God and tried to serve Him, something happened early in his presidency that profoundly transformed his life: Ronald Reagan came within a quarter of an inch of death. When he was shot on a Washington street in March 1981, the bullet came that close to his heart. So many things went miraculously right that day: The Secret Service agent protecting Dad quickly decided to take him to the hospital (when he arrived, doctors could not detect any blood pressure); the explosive-tipped bullet failed to explode; doctors just happened to be attending a staff meeting at the hospital when Dad was brought in—so all the institution's finest medical minds were on hand; the doctors found the bullet after hours of exploration—and just as they were ready*

*to give up looking for it. Few people realize how close he came to death—and how close the world came to losing a great man.*

*Dad's survival was a genuine miracle. As Cardinal Terence Cooke of New York told Dad during a visit to his hospital room, "Mr. President, you surely have an angel sitting on your shoulder."*

*Shortly after the assassination attempt, Dad talked with me about the profound change he had undergone—and the profound commitment he had made. "Michael," he said, "I look at all the things that could have gone wrong that day—yet God controlled every circumstance. I believe He spared me for a purpose. I want you to know, Michael, that I've made a decision to recommit the rest of my life, and the rest of my presidency, to God."*

*Here are some of the expressions of faith Ronald Reagan has made throughout his public life.*

What America needs is spiritual renewal and reconciliation—first, man with God, and then man with man.

*Campaign stump speech, 1976*

Going around this country, I have found a great hunger in America for a spiritual revival; for a belief that law must be based on a higher law; for a return to traditions and values that we once had. Our government, in its most sacred documents—the Constitution and the Declaration of Independence and all—

speak of man being created, of a Creator; that we're a nation under God.

*Reagan–Anderson presidential debate,*
*September 21, 1980*

Whatever happens now, I owe my life to God and will try to serve Him in every way I can.

*Diary entry after being released from the hospital following*
*the 1981 assassination attempt*

I've always believed that we were, each of us, put here for a reason, that there is a plan, somehow a divine plan for all of us. I know now that whatever days are left to me belong to Him.

*Annual National Prayer Breakfast*
*Washington, D.C., February 4, 1982*

Freedom prospers only where the blessings of God are avidly sought and humbly accepted.

*Annual convention of the*
*National Association of Evangelicals*
*Orlando, Florida, March 8, 1983*

While America's military strength is important, let me add here that I've always maintained that the struggle now going on for the world will never be decided by bombs or rockets, by armies or military might. The real crisis we face today is a spiritual one; at root, it is a test of moral will and faith.

*Annual convention of the*
*National Association of Evangelicals*
*Orlando, Florida, March 8, 1983*

Talking to a church audience like this reminds me a little of a church in a little town in Illinois—Dixon, Illinois—that I used to attend as a boy. One sweltering Sunday morning in July, the minister told us he was going to preach the shortest sermon he had ever given. And then he said a single sentence: "If you think it's hot today, just wait."

*Annual convention of the*
*National Association of Evangelicals*
*Columbus, Ohio, March 6, 1984*

Without God, there is no virtue, because there's no prompting of the conscience. Without God, we're mired in the material, that flat world that tells us only what the senses perceive. Without God, there is a coarsening of the society. And without God, democracy will not and cannot long endure. If we ever forget that we're one nation under God, then we will be a nation gone under.

*Speech at the Ecumenical Prayer Breakfast*
*Republican National Convention*
*Dallas, Texas, August 23, 1984*

It is inconceivable to me that anyone could accept this delegated authority without asking God's help. I pray that we who legislate and administer will be granted wisdom and strength beyond our own limited power; that with divine guidance we can avoid easy expedients, as we work to build a state where liberty under law and justice can triumph, where compassion can govern, and wherein the people can participate and prosper because of their government and not in spite of it.

*Speech as governor of California,*
*"California and the Problem of Government Growth"*
*January 5, 1967*

Sometimes when I'm faced with an unbeliever, an atheist, I am tempted to invite him to the greatest gourmet dinner that one could ever serve, and when we finished eating that magnificent dinner, to ask him if he believes there's a cook.

*May 30, 1988*

# FAMILY

Families stand at the center of society, so building our future must begin by preserving family values . . . In Washington everyone looks out for special interests groups. Well, I think families are pretty special. And with your help, will continue looking out for their interests.

*"The American Family," radio address to the nation*
*Camp David, Maryland, December 3, 1983*

When the liberals say "family," they mean "Big Brother in Washington." When we say "family," we mean "honor thy father and mother."

*Republican party rally*
*Waco, Texas, September 22, 1988*

We know that the secret of America's success has been our drive to excel, a spirit born and nurtured by our families. With their dreams and hard work, they've built our nation, made her

The Reagan family in the 1970s
Patti, Nancy, Dad, me, Maureen, and Ron Jr.

great, and kept her good. Everything we've accomplished began in those bedrock values parents have sought to impart throughout our history—values of faith in God, honesty, caring for others, personal responsibility, thrift, and initiative.

But families cannot prosper and keep America strong if government becomes a Goliath that preys upon their wealth, usurps their rights, and crushes their spirit. For too many years, overgrown government has stood in your way, taking more and more of what you earned, no matter how hard you tried.

*"Federal Income Taxation," radio address to the nation*
*Camp David, Maryland, April 9, 1983*

The right of parents and the rights of family take precedence over those of Washington-based bureaucrats and social engineers.

*Annual convention of the*
*National Association of Evangelicals*
*Orlando, Florida, March 8, 1983*

Dad fulfilling his football dreams at Eureka College in 1929

# FOOTBALL

*From the time he was a young boy, Ronald Reagan lived and dreamed the game of football. "Our house overlooked the high school playing field," he recalled in* An American Life, *"and I spent countless afternoons sitting on an earthen ledge watching and hearing the clash of padded bodies butting up against one another and dreaming of the day when I could put on a uniform and join the combat."*

*His dreams were fulfilled on the football fields of Dixon High and Eureka College. After college, as a radio broadcaster, he announced many football games for station WHO in Des Moines. In Hollywood he earned a place in movie history as George Gipp— the immortal Gipper—in* Knute Rockne, All American *(1940). Here are some quips and recollections about Dad's favorite sport.*

I couldn't play baseball because I couldn't see good enough. That's why I turned to football. The ball was bigger and so were the fellows.

*June 22, 1981*

I loved playing on the line: For me, it was probably a marriage made in heaven. It's as fundamental as anything in life—a collision between two bodies, one determined to advance, the other determined to resist; one man against another man, blocking, tackling, breaking through the line.

An American Life

*(New York: Simon & Schuster, 1990), pp. 39–40*

I was interviewed just the other day before I came out here by a reporter from the Bloomington *Pantagraph*, who came up and wanted to talk all about memories, Illinois and Eureka College and all. And then he said, "Well now, there's a story going around about you scoring a touchdown against Normal in the last minutes of play." And that just goes to show you how stories can get stretched. I can tell you about that touchdown.

We were one point ahead, as I remember. And there were just seconds to go. I'd been in the entire game, and Normal was passing, throwing bombs all over. Now remember, no one in our backfield was over about five nine or ten in those days, so our pass defense wasn't all it should be if anyone on the other side was taller than they were. I used to charge against my man and then when I felt it was going to be a pass, duck back into the secondary and see if I could help cover for passes.

And I saw everyone sucked over to one side of the field, and this Normal fellow—never forget that bright red jersey—was going down the field all by himself. And I took out after him. Pretty soon, as he was looking back, I knew the ball must be coming. And I turned around and here it came, and I went up in the air, I got it, but by this time, as I say, having been in the entire game, I knew that there wasn't anything left in me. There was a lineman's dream, a guard way over on the sideline, about 75 yards from the goal line but a clear field down that sideline. But coming down with the ball, I thought if I just juggle it for a second or two, he'll tackle me. We still win the ball game, and I won't have to run!

Well, I juggled it and I bent over, and I juggled it some more and nothing happened. And just as I started to raise my head, he put his arms around me and said, "Tag, you're it!"

At the same moment, I saw a substitute coming in for me. And I started for the sideline, and [coach] Ralph McKenzie, very serious of face—indeed, angry of face—said, "What happened to you?"

And all I could say was, "I'm tired!"

But that was my touchdown that was never made, my lineman's dream.

*Eureka College alumni dinner*
*Peoria, Illinois, May 9, 1982*

# *F*REEDOM

Freedom is a fragile thing and is never more than one generation away from extinction. It is not ours by inheritance; it must be fought for and defended constantly by each generation, for it comes only once to a people. Those who have known freedom and then lost it have never known it again.

*Speech as governor of California,*
*"California and the Problem of Government Growth"*
*January 5, 1967*

We stand here on the only island of freedom that is left in the whole world. There is no place to flee to . . . no place to escape to. We defend freedom here or it is gone. There is no place for us to run, only to make a stand. And if we fail, I think we face telling our children, and our children's children, what it was we found more precious than freedom. Because I am sure that someday— if we fail in this—there will be a generation that will ask.

*Quoted by Lou Cannon in* Ronnie and Jesse: A Political Odyssey
*(Garden City, New York: Doubleday, 1969), p. 68*

Dad campaigning in Liberty Park, New York, in 1980

Not too long ago, two friends of mine were talking to a Cuban refugee, a businessman who had escaped from Castro, and in the midst of his story one of my friends turned to the other and said, "We don't know how lucky we are." And the Cuban stopped and said, "How lucky you are! I had someplace to escape to." In that sentence he told us the entire story. If we lose freedom here, there is no place to escape to. This is the last stand on earth.

> *"A Time for Choosing" (a.k.a. "The Speech")*
> *Televised address to the nation on behalf of*
> *Barry Goldwater, October 27, 1964*

You and I know and do not believe that life is so dear and peace so sweet as to be purchased at the price of chains and slavery. If nothing is worth dying for, when did this begin—just in the face of this enemy? Or should Moses have told the children of Israel to live in slavery under the pharaohs? Should Christ have refused the cross? Should the patriots of Concord Bridge have thrown down their guns and refused to fire the shot heard round the world? The martyrs of history were not fools, and our honored dead who gave their lives to stop the advance of the Nazis didn't die in vain!

*"A Time for Choosing" (a.k.a. "The Speech")*
*Televised address to the nation on behalf of*
*Barry Goldwater, October 27, 1964*

Man is not free unless government is limited. There's a clear cause and effect here that is as neat and predictable as a law of physics: As government expands, liberty contracts.

*Farewell address, The Oval Office*
*January 11, 1989*

I don't know all the national anthems of the world, but I do know this: The only anthem of those I do know that ends with a question is ours, and may it be ever thus. Does that banner still wave "o'er the land of the free and the home of the brave?" Yes, it does, and we're going to see that it continues to wave over that kind of a country.

*"Salute to President Reagan" dinner, given by*
*the Republican Members of Congress*
*Washington, D.C., May 4, 1982*

The story is told that one night at dinner here at Mount Vernon, Lafayette said to Washington, "General, you Americans even in war and desperate times have a superb spirit. You're happy and you're confident. Why is it?"

And Washington answered, "There is freedom. There is space for a man to be alone and think, and there are friends who owe each other nothing but affection."

*Ceremony marking the 250th anniversary*
*of George Washington's birth*
*Mount Vernon, Virginia, February 22, 1982*

Four times in my lifetime, our soldiers have been sent overseas to fight in foreign lands. Their remains can be found from Flanders Field to the islands of the Pacific. Not once were those young men sent abroad in the cause of conquest. Not once did they come home claiming a single square inch of some other country as a trophy of war. A great danger in the past, however, has been the failure by our enemies to remember that while we Americans detest war, we love freedom and stand ready to sacrifice for it. We love freedom not only because it's practical and beneficial but because it is morally right and just.

*Televised address to the nation before*
*the U.S.–Soviet Summit in Geneva*
*Switzerland, The Oval Office, November 14, 1985*

# *T*HE FUTURE

*As a boy, growing up in the Great Depression, Ronald Reagan always had one foot in the future. He eagerly devoured Edgar Rice Burroughs' novels about the Martian adventures of earthman John Carter and his girlfriend, a Barsoomian princess named Deja Thoris. After coming to Hollywood, he enjoyed the science fiction adventure films and serials of the forties and fifties. He even starred in one of them—Murder in the Air (1940), in which he played Secret Service agent Brass Bancroft, who prevents foreign spies from stealing an American-made death ray projector that can shoot down enemy aircraft from a distance (shades of the Strategic Defense Initiative!).*

*Back in 1967 Ronald Reagan was invited by physicist Edward Teller to attend a briefing on defense technologies at the Lawrence Livermore National Laboratory in California. Teller, known as "the father of the hydrogen bomb," later recalled that the newly elected governor of California asked "good and fundamental questions" about the possibilities for an antimissile defense. Clearly the seeds of the Strategic Defense Initiative were planted long before Ronald Reagan went to the White House.*

*Even after he left office, Dad was fascinated by dreams of a bright future for humanity. In 1991 he stopped by Paramount Studios and watched the filming of an episode of* Star Trek: The Next Generation. *Between takes, Dad chatted with actor Patrick Stewart and producer Gene Roddenberry about the show and Roddenberry's optimistic vision of the future—an optimism that was in many ways similar to his own.*

*There is an unfair stereotype of older people as being hopelessly stuck in the past. Ronald Reagan shattered that stereotype. As governor of California, Dad once met with a group of students who complained his generation was out of touch. "You don't know what it's like," one student told him, "to grow up in an age of atomic bombs, space travel, and high-speed computers." And Dad replied, "You're right. My generation didn't grow up with such things. We invented them."*

*Here are some other typically Reaganesque observations on the future.*

If you want to know which way to go in the future, you have to know which path you took in the past and where you stepped in a gopher hole along the way.

*October 15, 1974*

For two hundred years we've lived in the future, believing that tomorrow would be better than today and today would be better than yesterday. I still believe that.

*The Reagan–Carter debate*
*October 28, 1980*

The dialogue and the deeds of the past few decades are not sufficient to the day in which we live. They cannot keep the promise of tomorrow. The encrusted bureaucracies and the ingrained procedures which have developed of late respond neither to the minority nor the majority. We've come to a turning point. We have a decision to make. Will we continue with yesterday's agenda and yesterday's failures, or will we reassert our ideals and our standards, will we reaffirm our faith, and renew our purpose? This is a time for choosing.

*Conservative Political Action Conference*
*Washington, D.C., March 20, 1981*

A fellow named James Allen once wrote in his diary, "Many thinking people believe America has seen its best days." He wrote that on July 26, 1775. There are still those who believe America is weakening; that our glory was the brief flash of time called the twentieth century; that ours was a burst of greatness too bright and brilliant to sustain; that America's purpose is past.

My friends, I utterly reject those views. That's not the

America we know. We were meant to be masters of destiny, not victims of fate. Who among us would trade America's future for that of any other country in the world? And who could possibly have so little faith in our America that they would trade our tomorrows for our yesterdays?

*Republican National Convention*
*Houston, Texas, August 17, 1992*

Remember this: When we come to the edge of our known world, we're standing on the shores of the infinite. Dip your hand in that limitless sea—you're touching the mystery of God's universe. Set sail across its waters and you embark on the boldest, most noble adventure of all. Out beyond our present horizons lie whole new continents of possibility, new worlds of hope waiting to be discovered. We've traveled far, but we've only begun our journey. There are hungry to feed, sicknesses to cure, and new worlds to explore. And this is no time for small plans or shrinking ambitions. We stand on the threshold of an epic age, an age of technological splendor and an explosion of human potential—an age for heroes. And I think I'm seeing many of them right here in this room.

*Reception for members of the Young Astronauts Program*
*Washington, D.C., June 11, 1986*

# GENERATIONS

There is a tendency in today's world to put more than years between us. Somehow, as humans, we have been stratified into a horizontal society instead of vertical. Layers of humanity are separated into age groups from preschool to those the social thinkers refer to as senior citizens. And somehow we are losing our ability to establish communications between layers. What is even worse, there is a growing hostility between these layers.

It is an unnatural situation. Humanity is vertically structured. The teenager will become the young married or junior executive and, in turn, the middle-aged and eventually the senior citizen. Each one of us will take his faults and virtues, his pluses and minuses, through the years, being at all times the sum total of all he has experienced.

This separation into horizontal layers makes no sense at all. What of this talk that no one over thirty understands the youth of today? If this is true, then what happens when you reach thirty? Do you suddenly join us and quit understanding those who have not quite reached the magic age?

Each generation is critical of its predecessor. As the day nears when classroom and playing field must give way to the larger arena with its problems of inequality and human misunderstanding, it is easy to look at those in that arena and demand to know why the problems remain unsolved. We who preceded you asked that question of those who preceded us, and another younger generation will ask it of you.

I hope there will be less justification for the question when it is your turn to answer. What I am trying to say is that no generation has failed completely, nor will yours succeed completely.

*"The Value of Understanding the Past"*
*Eureka College Library Dedication*
*September 28, 1967*

# $T$HE GIPPER

Dad in 1984
He truly was The Gipper.

*Without question Dad's best-known role was that of football star George Gipp, the immortal Gipper. His most famous scene in the movie occurs as the Gipper is dying from an advanced strep infection in his throat. With his last few breaths, the Gipper (Ronald Reagan) tells Notre Dame head coach Knute Rockne (Pat O'Brien):*

Someday, when things are tough, maybe you can ask the boys to go in there and win just one for the Gipper.

*We sometimes forget that this wasn't just a made-up scene in a movie. This touching moment is a reenactment of the actual dying words of the real-life Gipper to his real-life coach, Knute Rockne. Gipp—one of the greatest all-around players in college football history—had contracted the strep infection in Notre Dame's win over Northwestern. The deathbed conversation between Gipp and Rockne really did take place, just as it is depicted in the film. Only twenty-five years old, Gipp died on December 14, 1920. Coach Rockne listened to Gipp's last words—and he never forgot them.*

*Eight years later, when the underdog Fighting Irish of Notre Dame went to play unbeaten Army in Yankee Stadium, Rockne related the Gipper's last words in his pregame pep talk. "The day before he died," said Coach Rockne, "George Gipp asked me to wait until the situation seemed hopeless, then ask the team to go out and win one for the Gipper. Well, fellas, this is the day, and you are the team."*

*The Fighting Irish went out and won it, all right—12 to 6. Those who saw the game said it was the most amazing exhibition of inspired football ever played.*

*Now, what about you and me? Are we in the game? Or are we*

*on the sidelines? George Gipp went out and showed how it's done in the grid bowl, and that other Gipper, Ronald Reagan, showed how it's done in the arena of the world. But the job isn't finished. At the end of his presidency, he called on all of us to draw inspiration from him, to get in the game, and put our lives on the line—to win one for the Gipper. He said:*

I hope that someday your children and grandchildren will tell of the time that a certain president came to town at the end of a long journey and asked their parents and grandparents to join him in setting America on the course to the new millennium and that a century of peace, prosperity, opportunity, and hope had followed. So, if I could ask you just one last time: Tomorrow, when mountains greet the dawn, would you go out there and win one for the Gipper?

*Campaign rally for Vice President George Bush*
*San Diego, California, November 7, 1988*

# GOOD AND EVIL

Anatoly Sharansky was a Jewish dissident imprisoned in a vile gulag because he dared to speak out against Soviet persecution of the Jews. He could have easily won his release by signing a paper recanting his charges and calling the USSR a democracy that treated Jews well. Sharansky refused to sign—and so he remained in the gulag.

Sharansky was later traded to the West for a convicted Soviet spy. When he arrived in the United States, he went to the White House to meet Ronald Reagan. During that meeting, the Jewish dissident told my father, "Mr. President, whatever you do—do not tone down your speeches! Continue speaking the truth. When I was in the gulag, I lost all hope that I would ever see freedom and that the Soviet Union would ever fall. But while I was there, someone slipped a message to me on a tiny piece of paper. The message read, 'The American president, Ronald Reagan, has called the Soviet Union an evil empire.' Those words gave me hope."

The first two quotations that follow come from the very speech that gave Anatoly Sharansky hope in his hour of darkness—the infamous "Evil Empire" speech.

We must never forget that no government schemes are going to perfect man. We know that living in this world means dealing with what philosophers would call the phenomenology of evil or, as theologians would put it, the doctrine of sin. There is sin and evil in the world, and we're enjoined by Scripture and the Lord Jesus to oppose it with all our might.

*Annual convention of the*
*National Association of Evangelicals,*
*Orlando, Florida, March 8, 1983*

I urge you to beware the temptation of pride—the temptation of blithely declaring yourselves above it all and labeling both sides equally at fault, to ignore the facts of history and the aggressive impulses of an evil empire, to simply call the arms race a giant misunderstanding and thereby remove yourself from the struggle between right and wrong and good and evil.

*Annual convention of the*
*National Association of Evangelicals,*
*Orlando, Florida, March 8, 1983*

We've heard in our century far too much of the sounds of anguish from those who live under totalitarian rule. We've seen too many monuments made not out of marble or stone but out of barbed wire and terror. But from these terrible places have come survivors, witnesses to the triumph of the human spirit over the mystique of state power, prisoners whose spiritual values made them the rulers of their guards. With their survival, they brought us the secret of the camps, a lesson for our time and for any age: Evil is powerless if the good are unafraid.

*Conservative Political Action Conference*
*Washington, D.C., March 20, 1981*

Let us be frank. Evil still stalks the planet. Its ideology may be nothing more than bloodlust; no program more complex than economic plunder or military aggrandizement. But it is evil all the same. And wherever there are forces that would destroy the human spirit and diminish human potential, they must be recognized, and they must be countered.

*"Democracy's Next Battle"*
*Oxford Union Society*
*Oxford, England, December 4, 1992*

# GORBACHEV

Dad and Gorbachev ended the 1986 SALT negotiations
in Reykjavik, Iceland, on a sour note.

*The Reagan family was gathered in Dad's hotel suite the night the Republican convention nominated Gerald Ford in Kansas City, 1976. Afterward, Dad looked at me with a rueful grin and said, "You know what hurts the most about not getting the nomination?*

*It's that I really looked forward to becoming president and squaring off against the Russians at the SALT negotiations."*

*The threat of nuclear war was a major concern of Ronald Reagan's, and he was especially concerned about the many one-sided concessions America had made to the Soviets in the Strategic Arms Limitation Talks, which had been going on since 1969. "I wanted to sit down at that big conference table with the Russian Secretary General," he continued, "and I wanted to listen to all the Soviet demands, all the things the United States would have to give up in order to get along with the Russians. I was going to listen calmly, nodding and smiling—and then, when he had finished listing all his demands, I was going to get up from my chair, walk around to his side of the table, and whisper in his ear, 'Nyet.' I'm really sorry I won't get to say 'nyet' to the Soviets."*

*In October 1986—just a little more than ten years after losing the nomination to Gerald Ford—Ronald Reagan got his opportunity to say "nyet" to the Soviets. It was in Reykjavik, Iceland, at the second summit meeting between Ronald Reagan and Soviet leader Mikhail Gorbachev (they had previously met in Geneva, Switzerland). The two leaders had come very close to an agreement that would have dramatically reduced the nuclear arsenals of both nations, and they had talked realistically about the possibility of both sides eliminating all nuclear weapons! The talks were going so well that Dad and the rest of the U.S. delegation stayed an extra day to keep the momentum going.*

*But then came the moment my father had anticipated ten years earlier. Gorbachev laid the deal-breaker on the bargaining table—a condition that had not been mentioned in all the hours of talks that had occurred. Everything hinged, Gorbachev declared, on the United States stopping research and production of the Strategic Defense Initiative (SDI)—Dad's cherished hope for producing a world in which nukes would at last be obsolete.*

*Dad pointed out that it had always been his plan to share SDI technology with the Soviets, so that both sides would feel secure against nuclear attack. "How can we trust such a guarantee?" Gorbachev countered through his interpreter. "Once you have your antimissile defense in place, what is to prevent you from using it as a shield from which to launch a preemptive strike?"*

*Ronald Reagan answered in words to this effect: "In over two hundred years of American history, we have never started a fight. We have never fought a war of conquest. You are a student of history, Mr. Secretary General, and you know that the United States of America is the most peaceful, least warlike nation in modern history."*

*"You say your intentions are peaceful," Gorbachev countered. "But I can't gamble the security of the Soviet people on your say-so. We don't believe you."*

*"Well," Dad replied, "perhaps that's because you're judging America by the way your own country has behaved."*

*"Mr. President," said Gorbachev, "we have made great progress at this summit. We both want to see that progress continue. But it will all come to nothing unless the United States abandons SDI."*

*At that point, Gorbachev could see the anger in Dad's face—something few people ever see. Dad told him, "There's no way that's going to happen. We are committed to SDI."*

*With the negotiations at an impasse, the two men rose from the table. Gorbachev made one final attempt to absolve himself of responsibility for the failure of the talks. "I don't know what more I could have done," said the Soviet leader.*

*"I do," said Dad. "You could have said yes."*

*And that's how the Reykjavik summit ended.*

*As far as I know, Dad never went around the table and whispered "nyet" in Gorbachev's ear—but his reply to the Soviets was just as firm and clear as if he had. The grim-faced photographs taken at the conclusion of the summit show that both leaders were profoundly disappointed with the outcome of the talks. But history has shown that Ronald Reagan was wise to stand tall against Soviet pressure. America's commitment to SDI forced the Soviets into a crash research program of their own—and that was one of the factors that bankrupted and collapsed the evil empire.*

*Dad ultimately came to have great personal respect for Mikhail Gorbachev. More importantly, Gorbachev left Iceland with a heightened respect for Ronald Reagan—and for America's commitment to principle and the ideal of a world beyond nuclear blackmail.*

*Here are some of Ronald Reagan's personal reflections on Mikhail Gorbachev.*

The only reason I'd never met with General Secretary Gorbachev's predecessors was because they kept dying on me—Brezhnev, Chernenko, Andropov. Then along came Gorbachev. He was different in style, in substance, and, I believe, in intellect from previous Soviet leaders. He is a man who takes chances and that's what you need for progress. He is a remarkable force for change in that country.

We first met in Geneva. My team had set up a guesthouse away from the main meeting area where Gorbachev and I could talk one-on-one. He jumped at the chance when I suggested we sneak away. And there we sat and talked for hours in front of a roaring fire. I opened by telling him that ours was a unique situation—two men who together had the power to bring on World War III. By the same token we had the capability to bring about world peace. I said, "We don't mistrust each other because we're armed. We're armed because we mistrust each other." I asked him how, in addition to eliminating the arms, how could we eliminate the mistrust?

I did not know when I left for that meeting in Geneva, I would eventually call Mikhail Gorbachev a friend.

Speaking My Mind: Selected Speeches
*(New York: Simon & Schuster, 1989), pp. 247–248*

Gorbachev could be warm and outgoing in a social setting even though several hours earlier we'd had sharp differences of opinion; maybe there was a little of Tip O'Neill in him. He could tell jokes about himself and even about his country, and I grew to like him more.

*An American Life*
*(New York: Simon & Schuster, 1990), p. 639*

Both of us have advisers and assistants, but, you know, in the final analysis, the responsibility to preserve peace and increase cooperation is ours. Our people look to us for leadership and nobody can provide it if we don't. But we won't be very effective leaders unless we can rise above the specific but secondary concerns that preoccupy our respective bureaucracies and give our governments a strong push in the right direction.

*Letter to Soviet General Secretary Mikhail Gorbachev*
*November 28, 1985*

My view is that President Gorbachev is different from previous Soviet leaders. I think he knows some of the things wrong with his society and is trying to fix them. We wish him well. And we'll continue to work to make sure that the Soviet Union that eventually emerges from this process is a less threatening one. What it all boils down to is this: I want the new closeness to continue. And it will, as long as we make it clear that we will continue to act in a certain way as long as they continue to act in a helpful manner. If and when they don't, at first pull your punches. If they persist, pull the plug. It's still trust but verify. It's still play, but cut the cards. It's still watch closely. And don't be afraid to see what you see.

*Farewell address, The Oval Office*
*January 11, 1989*

# GOVERNMENT

*Ronald Reagan was praised by some and condemned by others for his so-called antigovernment views. But what does it mean to be "antigovernment"? There are many people in this country who say, "I love my country, but I hate my government." Is that possible? If you love your country, don't you have to love your government as well?*

*Apparently most Americans struggle with these questions. A survey conducted in March 1995 found that only 15 percent of Americans have "a great deal of faith" in the federal government. Amazingly, that is a full 30 points below the 45 percent level of confidence reported in a 1975 Gallup poll—immediately following Watergate and the resignation of Richard Nixon! Clearly many, if not most, Americans are disillusioned with their government these days. So Ronald Reagan's so-called antigovernment observations— both his humorous one-liners and his probing assessments—are as profound today as they were ten, twenty, and thirty years ago.*

★

Government's view of the economy could be summed up in a few short phrases: If it moves, tax it. If it keeps moving, regulate it. And if it stops moving, subsidize it.

*White House Conference on Small Business*
*August 15, 1986*

The government in Washington is spending some $7 million every minute I talk to you . . . If they'll stop spending, I'll stop talking.

*Campaign stump speech*
*May 1976*

Government is like a baby—an alimentary canal with a big appetite at one end and no sense of responsibility at the other.

*Speech before the Canadian Parliament*
*Ottawa, Canada, March 11, 1981*

★

The best view of big government is in the rearview mirror as we leave it behind.

*Spirit of America Rally*
*Atlanta, Georgia, January 26, 1984*

★

Once upon a time, the only contact you had with government was when you went to buy a stamp.

*California, 1965*

No government ever voluntarily reduces itself in size. Government programs, once launched, never disappear. Actually, a government bureau is the nearest thing to eternal life we'll ever see on this earth!

*"A Time for Choosing" (a.k.a. "The Speech")*
*Televised address to the nation on behalf of*
*Barry Goldwater, October 27, 1964*

Nothing lasts longer than a temporary government program.

*Speech at the Herbert Hoover Presidential Library*
*West Branch, Iowa, August 8, 1992*

If you want to make sure crime doesn't pay, let the government run it.

*California, 1967*

There seems to be an increasing awareness of something we Americans have known for some time—that the ten most dangerous words in the English language are "Hi, I'm from the government, and I'm here to help."

*Address to the Future Farmers of America*
*July 28, 1988*

★

Either you will control your government, or government will control you.

*"Why the Conservative Movement Is Growing"*
*Southern GOP Convention*
*Atlanta, Georgia, December 7, 1973*

★

For three decades we have sought to solve the problems of unemployment through government planning, and the more the plans fail, the more the planners plan . . . Well, now if government planning and welfare had the answer—and they've had almost thirty years of it—shouldn't we expect government to read the score to us once in a while? Shouldn't they be telling us about the decline each year in the number of people needing help? And the reduction in the need for public housing?

But the reverse is true.

*"A Time for Choosing" (a.k.a. "The Speech")*
*Televised address to the nation on behalf of*
*Barry Goldwater, October 27, 1964*

Public servants say, always with the best of intentions, "What greater service we could render if only we had a little more money and a little more power." But the truth is that outside of its legitimate function, government does nothing as well or as economically as the private sector.

*"A Time for Choosing" (a.k.a. "The Speech")*
*Televised address to the nation on behalf of*
*Barry Goldwater, October 27, 1964*

Remember that every government service, every offer of government-financed security, is paid for in the loss of personal freedom . . . In the days to come, whenever a voice is raised telling you to let the government do it, analyze very carefully to see whether the suggested service is worth the personal freedom which you must forego in return for such service.

There are many well-meaning people today who work at placing an economic floor beneath all of us so that no one shall exist below a certain level or standard of living, and certainly we don't quarrel with this. But look more closely and you may find that all too often these well-meaning people are building a ceiling above which no one shall be permitted to climb.

Between the two, they are pressing us all into conformity, into a mold of standardized mediocrity.

*Commencement address*
*Eureka College, June 7, 1957*

In some dim beginning, man created the institution of government as a convenience for himself. And ever since that time, government has been doing its best to become an inconvenience.

*Speech before the U.S. Chamber of Commerce*
*September 24, 1972*

Over the past decades we've talked of curtailing government spending so that we can then lower the tax burden. Sometimes we've even taken a run at doing that. But there were always those who told us that taxes couldn't be cut until spending was reduced. Well you know, we can lecture our children about extravagance until we run out of voice and breath. Or we can cure their extravagance by simply reducing their allowance.

*Televised address on the Economy*
*The Oval Office*
*February 5, 1981*

# *H*ISTORY

History will ask and our answer will determine the fate of freedom for a thousand years. Did a nation born of hope lose hope? Did a people forged by courage find courage wanting? Did a generation steeled by hard war and a harsh peace forsake honor at the moment of great climactic struggle for the human spirit?

*May 17, 1981*

My young friends, history is a river that may take us as it will. But we have the power to navigate, to choose direction, and make our passage together.

*April 30, 1984*

My friends, we live in a world that is lit by lightning. So much is changing and will change, but so much endures and transcends time. History is a ribbon, always unfurling; history is a journey.

*Second inaugural address*
*January 21, 1985*

★

I know it is something of a cliché to draw a parallel between the rise and fall of Rome and our own republic. Certainly, in academic circles, this is so, and yet the parallel is there in such detail as to be almost eerie . . .

The history of the Roman Empire has been better recorded and documented than almost all of the great civilizations of the past. We know it started with a kind of pioneer heritage not unlike our own. Then it entered into its two centuries of greatness, reaching its height in the second of those two centuries, going into its decline and collapse in the third. However, the signs of decay were becoming apparent in the latter years of that second century.

We are approaching the end of our second century. It has been pointed out that the days of democracy are numbered once the belly takes command of the head. When the less affluent feel the urge to break a commandment and begin to covet that which their more affluent neighbors possess, they are tempted to use their votes to obtain instant satisfaction. Then equal opportunity at the starting line becomes an extended guarantee of at least a tie at the finish of the race. Under the euphemism "the greatest good for the greatest number," we destroy a system which has accomplished just that and move toward the managed economy which strangles freedom and mortgages generations yet to come.

*Eisenhower College fund-raiser speech*
*October 14, 1969*

I feel certain that, despite all the challenges that beset us, this nation of freedom will flourish. But if we're to succeed in the future, we must first learn our own past. We must learn to go to a building like this and hear the echoes and sense the greatness and draw strength. For to study American history is, in a sense, to study free will. It is to see that all our greatness has been built up by specific acts of choice and determination. And it is to see how very fragile our nation is, how very quickly so much that we cherish could be lost.

*Address to the We the People organization*
*Philadelphia, Pennsylvania, April 1, 1987*

# *H*ORSES

There's nothing as good for the inside of a man as the outside of a horse.

*Said on many occasions*

There's something about the wild scenery and serenity at the ranch and having a horse between my knees that makes it easier to sort out a problem. I think people who haven't tried it might be surprised at how easily your thoughts can come together when you're on the back of a horse riding with nothing else to do but think about a decision that's ahead of you.

An American Life
*(New York: Simon & Schuster, 1990), p. 195*

*Once, as governor of California, someone suggested to Dad that he might build rapport with the young people if he rode a motorcycle. His reply:*

I'll have to stick to horseback riding. You see, there is the matter of security. When I go anyplace, I'm one of a group. We might look like Hell's Angels with all of us out there on motorcycles.

Dad relaxing on his ranch in 1986
He loves his horses.

# HUMILITY

*Humility is a virtue that is not highly prized in our society today, but Ronald Reagan possessed it as president—and that, in large part, was the source of his greatness.*

*Typical of his humility was his self-deprecating sense of humor. If you listened closely, you realized that even while he was lampooning a political opponent, the joke was really on himself. For example, when he heard that Alan Cranston (who was a few years younger than Dad) was running in the Democratic primary, Dad's response was, "Imagine running for president at his age!" And then there was his line about another Democratic hopeful, Gary Hart: "This country would never accept a president who looks like a movie star."*

*Dad never saw himself as superior to anyone else, even when he was the leader of the Free World. A few days after he was shot in early 1981, Vice President Bush visited him at the hospital, accompanied by several White House aides. But Dad wasn't in the bed. They called for him—and then they heard his voice coming from the bathroom.*

*"In here, fellas," said Dad. George Bush and the other men*

*found the president of the United States on his hands and knees on the cold tile floor, mopping up some water under the sink.*

*"What are you doing down there?" asked Bush, aghast.*

*"Well," said Dad, "they wouldn't let me take a bath, so I was giving myself a sponge bath. I guess I sort of made a mess of things."*

*"You should let the nurse clean that up," said Bush.*

*"Oh, this is my mess," said Dad. "I'd hate for the nurse to have to clean it up. Could you guys get me some more towels?"*

*Now, that's humility. Here are some other remarks that illustrate the humble heart of Ronald Reagan.*

A member of my staff who's been reviewing some of the videotapes of the campaign asked me the other day if you can feel an audience's adulation. I said that, yes, you could. (In fact, I bet I have a better idea of what it feels like to be a rock star than most twenty-year-olds.) So then he said, "Well, how do you handle it?" I said, "I pray that I will be deserving."

Speaking My Mind: Selected Speeches
*(New York: Simon & Schuster, 1989), p. 199*

It's an honor to have you all here at the White House. Now, I know that must sound strange. Most people think of it as an honor to be invited here, and that includes myself. I remember how humble I felt on that day in 1980 when the American people first asked me to come here.

*Ceremony honoring citizens who responded*
*heroically to a train wreck in Chase, Maryland*
*The White House, February 3, 1987*

[During the 1980s] I won a nickname, the Great Communicator. But I never thought it was my style or the words I used that made a difference: it was the content. I wasn't a great communicator, but I communicated great things, and they didn't spring full bloom from my brow, they came from the heart of a great nation—from our experience, our wisdom, and our belief in the principles that have guided us for two centuries.

*Farewell address, The Oval Office*
*January 11, 1989*

# $T$HE IRISH

*Dad's sense of humor is typically Irish—irreverent yet gentle, directed toward himself as much as to the next guy—equal parts wisdom and blarney.*

Because of the Irish, America today is a richer, freer, and, yes, a bit noisier land than it otherwise would have been.

*St. Patrick's Day radio address to the nation*
*Camp David, Maryland, March 17, 1984*

And may I conclude with a little Irish blessing—although, some suggest it's a curse: May those who love us, love us. And those who don't love us, may God turn their hearts. And if He doesn't turn their hearts, may He turn their ankles so we'll know them by their limping.

*Address on administration goals to senior presidential appointees*
*Washington, D.C., September 8, 1987*

★

Mr. Minister, Mr. Ambassador, Mrs. Donlon, honored guests . . . I'm honored to have received your traditional shamrocks, which symbolize this day and the friendship between our two countries. And I'm especially pleased and most grateful for the beautiful scroll of the Reagan family tree. Up on the Hill this morning, at a meeting with some of the legislative leadership, Senator Laxalt presented me with a great green button that he thought I should wear, which said, "Honorary Irishman." And I said to that son of the Basques, "I'm not honorary; I am." And now I have the proof of it here.

I am deeply grateful for this because my father was orphaned at age six, and I grew up never having heard anything or knowing anything about my family tree, and I would meet other people of the name Reagan or Regan—we're all of the same clan, all cousins, but I tried to say to the secretary [Treasury Secretary Donald Regan] one day that his branch of the family just couldn't handle that many letters. Then I received a letter or a paper from Ireland that told me that in the clan to which we belong, those who said Regan and spelled it that way were the professional people and the educators, and only the common laborers called it Reagan. So, meet a common laborer.

But anyway, I am delighted now finally to know what I've never known all my life—the line and the heritage and to where it goes in Ireland. My father also, at the same time, used to tell me and my brother when we were boys—very proudly he would say that in this country the Irish built the jails and then filled them. And I was kind of disturbed at the note of pride in his voice because I'd pictured this in a little different way until I finally learned what he was implying: that the great percentage of the police officers in our land are Irish.

*Luncheon with Ireland's ambassador, Sean Donlon*
*Washington, D.C., March 17, 1981*

During a trip to Ireland we visited Cashel Rock where St. Patrick is said to have raised the first cross. A young Irish guide was showing us through the ruins of an ancient cemetery. We came to a great tombstone, and chiseled in the stone was an inscription. It read: "Remember me as you pass by, for as you are, so once was I. But as I am you, too, will be. So be content to follow me." That was too much for some Irishman, who had scratched in the stone underneath, "To follow you I am content. I wish I knew which way you went."

*Amoco Corporation Annual Conference*
*New Orleans, Louisiana, March 17, 1992*

# JELLY BEANS

*Dad's fondness for jelly beans is famous. As governor of California during the energy crisis of the mid-1970s, he once remarked:*

There is no energy shortage here in California. We run the government on *jelly beans*!

*Of all the various sectors of the American economy that prospered during his presidency, it was undoubtedly the jelly bean industry that made the greatest gains of all. It is said that jelly bean sales in America increased tenfold during the Reagan '80s.*

*Early in his presidency, Dad hosted a White House luncheon with state legislators and county executives from around the country. There were supposed to be little paper cups of jelly beans at every table. Apparently one table got missed, prompting someone at that table to ask, during the question-and-answer session, "Where are the jelly beans?" Dad's reply:*

Say, they left your table without any? That's unfair . . .

I have to say that when I arrived [at the White House], there was a big jar in the middle of the cabinet table, and [the White House cabinet members ate them] faster than the cabinet in California. You should see them going around—passing them as they keep right on talking and arguing. As I've said, there's something of character reading you get in there because there's that fellow who, every once in a while, while he's picking them out all the same color, one at a time, passing them on—

But the man who delivers them just told me, he gave me a message about how properly to eat them. When I told him that I put three or four different colored ones in my mouth at the same time, [he said] they now have a recipe for eating them. You're supposed to put certain colors together, and then that will create a new flavor. Like lemon meringue pie or something.

I tell you, next thing you know, we'll have an agency regulating the eating of jelly beans!

*The White House, February 9, 1981*

# $L$EADERSHIP

Dad in 1984
How appropriate for him to stand under the banner of leadership

*If there's one subject Ronald Reagan can speak about with authority, it's leadership. Late in his presidency, he gave this prescription for successful leadership in an interview with a leading business journal:*

Surround yourself with the best people you can find, delegate authority, and don't interfere.

*Interview with* Fortune *magazine*
*September 15, 1986*

*That prescription will serve you well whether you are the CEO of a small widget-manufacturing company, the CEO of a Fortune 500 corporate giant, or the CEO of the most powerful nation on earth. Here are some other statements Ronald Reagan made on the importance of strong leadership on the national and world stage.*

It's hard, when you're up to your armpits in alligators, to remember you came here to drain the swamp.

*Talk to the administration's female appointees*
*The White House, February 10, 1982*

A leader, once convinced a particular course of action is the right one, must have the determination to stick with it and be undaunted when the going gets rough.

*Speech before the Cambridge Union Society*
*Cambridge, England, December 5, 1990*

After watching the State of the Union address the other night, I'm reminded of the old adage that imitation is the sincerest form of flattery. Only in this case, it's not flattery, but grand larceny—the intellectual theft of ideas that you and I recognize as our own. Speech delivery counts for little on the world stage unless you have convictions and, yes, the vision to see beyond the front row seats. The Democrats may remember their lines, but how quickly they forget the lessons of the past. I have witnessed five major wars in my lifetime, and I know how swiftly storm clouds can gather on a peaceful horizon. The next time a Saddam Hussein takes over a Kuwait, or North Korea brandishes a nuclear weapon, will we be ready to respond?

In the end it all comes down to leadership. That is what this country is looking for now. It was leadership here at home that gave us strong American influence abroad and the collapse of imperial communism. Great nations have responsibilities to lead, and we should always be cautious of those who would lower our profile, because they might just wind up lowering our flag.

*Republican National Committee Annual Gala*
*(celebrating Ronald Reagan's eighty-third birthday)*
*Washington, D.C., February 3, 1994*

# *L*IBERALS AND LIBERALISM

I have come to realize that a great many so-called liberals aren't liberal—they will defend to the death your right to agree with them.

> Where's the Rest of Me?
> *(New York: Dell, 1965, 1981)*

Yet anytime you and I question the schemes of the do-gooders, we are denounced as being against their humanitarian goals. They say we are always "against" things, never "for" anything. Well, the trouble with our liberal friends is not that they are ignorant, but that they know so much that isn't so!

> *"A Time for Choosing" (a.k.a. "The Speech")*
> *Televised address to the nation on behalf of*
> *Barry Goldwater, October 27, 1964*

Our task is far from over. Our friends in the other party will never forgive us for our success and are doing everything in their power to rewrite history. Listening to the liberals, you'd think that the 1980s were the worst period since the Great Depression, filled with suffering and despair. I don't know about you, but I'm getting awfully tired of the whining voices from the White House these days. They're claiming there was a decade of greed and neglect, but you and I know better than that. We were there.

*Republican National Committee Annual Gala*
*(celebrating Ronald Reagan's eighty-third birthday)*
*Washington, D.C., February 3, 1994*

# LIFE

Life is just one grand, sweet song, so start the music.

*Quote under Ronald Reagan's*
*picture in his high school yearbook,*
The Dixonian *(Class of '28)*

We make a living by what we get; we make a life by what we give.

*Speech at the Herbert Hoover Presidential Library*
*West Branch, Iowa, August 8, 1992*

# MARRIAGE

*In June 1971 I married a young woman who was eighteen years old and fresh out of high school. I was twenty-six and no more mature than she was. The marriage took place in Hawaii, and Dad did not attend. But just a few days before the wedding, I received a letter from him. It was straight from Dad's heart—honest, old-fashioned, and wise. I cried when I read it, and I've read it many times in the years since then.*

*My first marriage didn't last. But four years later, on November 7, 1975, I married Colleen. I can't imagine what I would have done or where I would have ended up without her. I have committed myself to living out the wise advice from my father's letter every day of my marriage to Colleen. Here is what Dad wrote.*

Dear Mike:

You've heard all the jokes that have been rousted around by all the "unhappy marrieds" and cynics. Now, in case no one has suggested it, there is another viewpoint. You have entered into the most meaningful relationship there is in all human life. It can be whatever you decide to make it.

Some men feel their masculinity can only be proven if they play out in their own life all the locker-room stories, smugly confident that what a wife doesn't know won't hurt her. The truth is, somehow, way down inside, without her ever finding lipstick on the collar or catching a man in the flimsy excuse of where he was till three A.M., a wife does know, and with that knowing, some of the magic of this relationship disappears. There are more men griping about marriage who kicked the whole thing away themselves than there can ever be wives deserving of blame.

There is an old law of physics that you can only get out of a thing as much as you put in it. The man who puts into the marriage only half of what he owns will get that out. Sure, there will be moments when you will see someone or think back on an earlier time and you will be challenged to see if you can still make the grade, but let me tell you how really great is the challenge of proving your masculinity and charm with one woman for the rest of your life. Any man can find a twerp here and there who will go along with cheating, and it doesn't take all that much manhood. It does take quite a man to remain attractive and to be loved by a woman who has heard him snore, seen him unshaven, tended him while he was sick, and washed his dirty underwear. Do that and keep her still feeling a warm glow and you will know some very beautiful music.

If you truly love a girl, you shouldn't ever want her to feel, when she sees you greet a secretary or a girl you both know, that humiliation of wondering if she was someone who caused you to be late coming home, nor should you want any other woman to be able to meet your wife and know she was smiling behind her eyes as she looked at her, the woman you love, remembering this was the woman you rejected even momentarily for her favors.

Mike, you know better than many what an unhappy home is and what it can do to others. Now you have a chance to make it come out the way it should. There is no greater happiness for a man than approaching a door at the end of a day knowing someone on the other side of that door is waiting for the sound of his footsteps.

Love, Dad

P.S. You'll never get in trouble if you say "I love you" at least once a day.

# MEMORIALS

Dad and Nancy walk among the memorial crosses at Normandy in 1984 during services for the fiftieth anniversary of D day.

*Certainly the most difficult task of the presidency is that of offering comfort in times of tragedy. During his eight years as president, Ronald Reagan was called upon a number of times to bring us together at times of national mourning—or to lead the nation in memorializing the past heroic sacrifices of Americans in times of war and national emergency.*

*Among the tragedies and losses Ronald Reagan memorialized as president were the loss of the space shuttle* Challenger, *the deadly missile firing against the USS* Stark, *the fortieth anniversary of D day, and the military plane crash in Newfoundland, December 12, 1985, that killed a planeload of soldiers on their way home for the holidays.*

*During such times, Ronald Reagan brought us all together, because the words he expressed came straight from the genuine anguish and love in his heart.*

All of these men were different, but they shared this in common: They loved America very much. There was nothing they wouldn't do for her. And they loved with the sureness of the young.

*Arlington Cemetery, May 25, 1986*

We stand on a lonely, windswept point on the northern shore of France. The air is soft, but forty years ago at this moment, the air was dense with smoke and the cries of men, and the air was filled with the crack of rifle fire and the roar of cannon. At dawn, on the morning of the sixth of June 1944, two-hundred and twenty-five Rangers jumped off the British landing craft and ran to the bottom of these cliffs. Their mission was one of the most difficult and daring of the invasion: to climb these sheer and desolate cliffs and take out the enemy guns. The Allies had been told that some of the mightiest of these guns were here and they would be trained on the beaches to stop the Allied advance.

The Rangers looked up and saw the enemy soldiers—at the edge of the cliffs, shooting down at them with machine guns and throwing grenades. And the American Rangers began to climb. They shot rope ladders over the face of these cliffs and began to pull themselves up. When one Ranger fell, another would take his place. When one rope was cut, a Ranger would grab another and begin his climb again. They climbed, shot back, and held their footing. Soon, one by one, the Rangers pulled themselves over the top, and in seizing the firm land at the top of these cliffs, they began to seize back the continent of Europe. Two-hundred and twenty-five came here. After two days of fighting only ninety could still bear arms.

Behind me is a memorial that symbolizes the Ranger daggers that were thrust into the top of these cliffs. And before me are the men who put them there.

These are the boys of Pointe du Hoc. These are the men who took the cliffs. These are the champions who helped free a continent. These are the heroes who helped end a war.

*Memorial address at Pointe du Hoc, Normandy, France*
*The fortieth anniversary of D day, June 6, 1984*

The crew of the space shuttle *Challenger* honored us by the manner in which they lived their lives. We will never forget them nor the last time we saw them, this morning, as they prepared for their journey and waved good-bye and "slipped the surly bonds of earth" to "touch the face of God."

*Televised address to the nation after the explosion of*
*the space shuttle* Challenger, *The Oval Office*
*January 28, 1986*

Our young friends—

Yes, young friends, for in our hearts you will always be young, full of the love that is youth—love of life, love of joy, love of country. You fought for your country and for its safety and for the freedom of others with strength and courage. We love you for it. We honor you. And we have faith that, as He does all His sacred children, the Lord will bless you and keep you, the Lord will make His face to shine upon you and give you peace, now and forevermore.

*Ronald and Nancy Reagan*
*Handwritten note left at the Vietnam Veterans Memorial*
*Veterans Day, November 11, 1988*

# MORALITY

No government at any level and for any price can afford the police necessary to assure our safety and our freedom unless the overwhelming majority of us are guided by an inner personal code of morality.

*Eisenhower College fund-raiser speech*
*October 14, 1969*

★

They say the world has become too complex for simple answers. They are wrong. There are no easy answers, but there are simple answers. We must have the courage to do what we know is morally right.

*"A Time for Choosing" (a.k.a. "The Speech")*
*Televised address to the nation on behalf of*
*Barry Goldwater, October 27, 1964*

Politics and morality are inseparable. And as morality's foundation is religion, religion and politics are necessarily related. We need religion as a guide. We need it because we are imperfect, and our government needs the church, because only those humble enough to admit they're sinners can bring to democracy the tolerance it requires in order to survive.

*Address before the Ecumenical Prayer Breakfast*
*Republican National Convention,*
*Dallas, Texas, August 23, 1984*

Dad and Nancy in the early 1950s

*In 1971, while he was governor of California, a reporter asked Dad to recall the nicest thing a girl ever did for him. His reply:*

The nicest thing a girl ever did for me was when a girl named Nancy married me and brought a warmth and joy to my life that has grown with each passing year. I know she won't mind if I add that the second nicest thing was a letter from a little fifth grade girl I received last week. She added a P.S., "You devil, you." I've walked with a swagger ever since.

*On election day 1980, Dad and Nancy walked into the polling place in Pacific Palisades—a private home where voting booths had been set up. It was the same cozy house in which citizen Ronald Reagan had voted in every election for the preceding twenty-five years. The election workers had a jar of jelly beans on the table, and Dad helped himself to a handful, then he and Nancy went into their respective booths and exercised one of the most precious of all American rights.*

*On their way out of the polling place, Dad and Nancy were besieged by reporters and photographers. One of them jokingly asked Dad, "Who did you vote for?"*

*His reply:* I voted for Nancy!

*Another reporter called out, "Who did she vote for?"*

*Dad's reply:* Oh, Nancy voted for some has-been actor!

*In 1988 my sister Maureen organized a luncheon at the Republican National Convention to honor Nancy Reagan and raise money for her campaign against drug abuse. The honor was a total surprise to Nancy, and Dad called her to the podium as he gave her an affectionate tribute straight from the heart. Of all the public speeches Dad ever gave, I think he enjoyed this one the most:*

What do you say about someone who gives your life meaning? What do you say about someone who's always there with support and understanding, someone who makes sacrifices so that your life will be easier and more successful? Well, what you say is that you love that person and treasure her.

I simply can't imagine the last eight years without Nancy . . . You know, she once said that a president has all kinds of advisers and experts who look after his interests when it comes to foreign policy or the economy or whatever, but no one who looks after his needs as a human being. Well, Nancy has done that for me through recuperations and crises. Every president should be so lucky.

I think it's all too common in marriages that, no matter how much partners love each other, they don't thank each other enough. And I suppose I don't thank Nancy enough for all that she does for me. So, Nancy, in front of all your friends here today, let me say, thank you for all you do. Thank you for your love. And thank you for just being you.

*Luncheon in honor of First Lady Nancy Reagan*
*Republican National Convention*
*New Orleans, Louisiana, August 15, 1988*

# NEIGHBORS

Remember the parable of the Good Samaritan? He crossed the road, knelt down, and bound up the wounds of the beaten traveler, the pilgrim, and then carried him into the nearest town. He didn't just hurry on by into town and then look up a caseworker and tell him there was a fellow back out on the road that looked like he might need help.

Isn't it time for us to get personally involved, for our churches and synagogues to restore our spirit of neighbor caring for neighbor? . . . We should be doing God's work on earth. We'll never find every answer, solve every problem, or heal every wound, but we can do a lot if we walk together down that one path that we know provides real hope.

*Annual National Prayer Breakfast*
*Washington, D.C., February 4, 1982*

# PATIENCE

*By now everyone knows Ronald Reagan's favorite story—the one about the parents with the overly optimistic son. In an effort to make a realist out of the boy, they placed him in a stable full of horse manure and ordered him to shovel it out. When they came back to check his progress, the parents expected him to be miserable, tired, and cured of his optimism. Instead, they found him whistling cheerfully as he happily shoveled his way through the mountain of manure. "Why," they asked the boy, "are you so happy?"*

*"Well, with all this manure around," the boy replied, "there's gotta be a pony in here somewhere!"*

*Do you know that boy's name? I'd bet the ranch his name is Ronald Reagan. I have personally watched Dad shovel out horse stalls—and I can tell you for a fact that he whistles like a lark with every shovelful.*

★

Years ago Nancy and I acquired a ranch that was in a state of some disrepair and neglect. It had a barn with eight stalls in it in which the previous owners had kept cattle. We planned to keep horses. So I went in those stalls, day after day. With a pick and a shovel, I lowered the level of those stalls, which had accumulated over the years. It took time and patience and a lot of work. What's true in a horse stall is just as true in life and in politics: You cannot undo in a few days or weeks what has taken years to accumulate.

*Told on various occasions*

Die-hard conservatives thought that if I couldn't get everything I asked for, I would jump off the cliff with the flag flying—go down in flames. No, if I can get seventy or eighty percent of what it is I'm trying to get . . . I'll take that and then continue to try to get the rest in the future.

*Quoted in* The New York Times, *October 6, 1985*

# $P$EACE

Dad and Gorbachev started out as cold war opponents and ended up friends.

*Ronald Reagan's detractors on the left tried to caricature him as a trigger-happy gunslinger who would drag America—and the whole world—into the cataclysm of war. Eight years of his peace-through-strength defense policy proved that this "gunslinger" was one of the greatest men of peace our century has seen. He never received the*

*Nobel Peace Prize, but I know he truly earned the Lord's affirmation from Matthew 5:9, "Blessed are the peacemakers, for they shall be called sons of God."*

We desire peace. But peace is a goal, not a policy. Lasting peace is what we hope for at the end of our journey. It doesn't describe the steps we must take nor the paths we should follow to reach that goal.

*Address to the nation on*
*strategic arms reduction and nuclear deterrence*
*November 22, 1982*

When we speak of peace, we should not mean just the absence of war. True peace rests on the pillars of individual freedom, human rights, national self-determination, and respect for the rule of law.

*Televised address to the nation before*
*the U.S.–Soviet Summit in Geneva*
*The Oval Office, November 14, 1985*

★

We intend to keep the peace—we will also keep our freedom.
*First State of the Union address, January 26, 1982*

A grade school class in Somerville, Massachusetts, recently wrote me to say, "We studied about countries and found out that each country in our world is beautiful and that we need each other. People may look a little different, but we're still people who need the same things." They said, "We want peace. We want to take care of one another. We want to be able to get along with one another. We want to be able to share. We want freedom and justice. We want to be friends. We want no wars. We want to be able to talk to one another. We want to be able to travel around the world without fear."

And then they asked, "Do you think that we can have these things one day?" Well, I do. I really do. Nearly two thousand years after the coming of the Prince of Peace, such simple wishes may still seem far from fulfillment. But we can achieve them. We must never stop trying.

*"Easter and Passover," radio address to the nation*
*Rancho del Cielo, California, April 2, 1983*

People don't make wars; governments do. And too many Soviet and American citizens have already shed too much blood because of violence by governments. The American people want less confrontation and more communication and cooperation, more opportunity to correspond, to speak freely with all people over our respective radio and television programs, and, most important, to visit each other in our homes so we could better understand your countries and you could know the truth about America . . .

May I just say—and I speak not only as the president of the United States but also as a husband, a father, a grandfather, and as a person who loves God and whose heart yearns deeply for a better future—my dream is for our peoples to come together in a spirit of faith and friendship, to help build and leave behind a far safer world.

*"Peace," radio address to the world from the broadcast studios*
*of Voice of America in Washington, D.C., September 24, 1983,*
*carried live on the VOA worldwide network and*
*simultaneously translated into some forty languages*

# POLITICS AND POLITICIANS

When Pat Brown commissioned a television commercial in which he told a group of small children, "I'm running against an actor, and you know who killed Abe Lincoln, don't you?," I knew he knew he was in trouble.

An American Life
*(New York: Simon & Schuster, 1990), p. 148*

Professional politicians like to talk about the value of experience in government. Nuts! The only experience you gain in politics is how to be political.

*1976*

Politics is supposed to be the second oldest profession. I have come to realize that it bears a very close resemblance to the first.

*Speech at a business conference*
*Los Angeles, California, March 2, 1977*

Politics is just like show business. You need a big opening. Then you coast for a while. Then you need a big finish.

*California, 1966*

I have learned that one of the most important rules in politics is poise—which means looking like an owl after you have behaved like a jackass.

*August 9, 1973*

I hope our political victory will be remembered as a generous one and our time in power will be recalled for the tolerance we showed for those with whom we disagree.

*Conservative Political Action Conference*
*Washington, D.C., March 20, 1981*

An evangelical minister and a politician arrived at heaven's gate one day together. And St. Peter, after doing all the necessary formalities, took them in hand to show them where their quarters would be. And he took them to a small, single room with a bed, a chair, and a table and said this was for the clergyman. And the politician was a little worried about what might be in store for him. And he couldn't believe it then when St. Peter stopped in front of a beautiful mansion with lovely grounds, many servants, and told him that these would be his quarters.

And he couldn't help but ask, "But wait— How—? There's something wrong—! Why do I get this mansion while that good and holy man only gets a single room?"

And St. Peter said, "You have to understand how things are up here. We've got thousands and thousands of clergy. You're the first politician who ever made it."

*Annual convention of the*
*National Association of Evangelicals,*
*Orlando, Florida, March 8, 1983*

# *P*OVERTY

Seventy-five years ago I was born in Tampico, Illinois, in a little flat above the bank building. We didn't have any other contact with the bank than that.

*February 6, 1986*

We were poor when I was young, but the difference then was that the government didn't come around telling you you were poor.

*July 6, 1986*

Our family didn't exactly come from the wrong side of the tracks, but we were certainly always within the sound of the train whistles.

*Said on more than one occasion*

Free enterprise has done more to reduce poverty than all the government programs dreamed up by Democrats.

*Speech as governor of California, 1972*

My friends, some years ago the federal government declared war on poverty—and poverty won.

*State of the Union address*
*January 25, 1988*

We are a humane and generous people and we accept without reservation our obligation to help the aged, disabled, and those unfortunates who, through no fault of their own, must depend on their fellow man. But we are not going to perpetuate poverty by substituting a permanent dole for a paycheck. There is no humanity or charity in destroying self-reliance, dignity, and self-respect—the very substance of moral fiber.

*"California and the Problem of Government Growth"*
*Speech as governor of California,*
*January 5, 1967*

# PRAYER

Dad is sworn in as governor of California in 1967.

*Ronald Reagan has long been a big believer in the power of prayer. He often said he could feel the prayers of the nation raising him back to health after the assassination attempt in 1981. And when he was governor of California, he experienced what he says could only be a miracle of God's healing power, released through prayer.*

*Shortly after his inauguration as governor, Dad was diagnosed with an ulcer. For over a year he avoided spicy foods, chugalugged Maalox, and prayed daily for healing—but no healing came. In fact the pain in his stomach got worse with time and the increasing pressures of the job.*

*One morning he got out of bed, went to the medicine cabinet, and took down the bottle of Maalox. Then a thought occurred to him:* You don't need to take this stuff. *He had no idea where that thought came from, but he decided to listen to it and forego his usual Maalox pick-me-up.*

*As he began his workday in the governor's office, he noticed that the ache in his stomach was gone. One of his early appointments that day was with a businessman from Southern California. They talked for a while about the man's concerns, then, as the man was about to leave, he turned to Ronald Reagan and said, "Governor, I just want you to know that I'm part of a group of believers who pray every day for you."*

*"Well," Dad replied, "I sure can use it. Thank you for your prayers."*

*Later that day, another businessman came in for an appointment— and this meeting ended the same way, with the man telling Dad that he was part of a prayer group that regularly prayed for the governor. A few days later, Dad went to his doctor for his regular checkup—and the doctor was astonished and unable to explain the fact that there was no sign of an ulcer. Dad was healed.*

*Does Ronald Reagan believe in the power of prayer? You bet he does! Here are some of his thoughts on prayer.*

I'll confess that I've been a little afraid to suggest what I'm going to suggest, what I'm going to say. But I'm more afraid not to. Can we begin our crusade joined together in a moment of silent prayer?

*[The audience rises, with heads bowed, for a few silent moments, after which Ronald Reagan concludes:]*

God bless America!

*Republican National Convention*
*Detroit, Michigan, July 17, 1980*

I am told that tens of thousands of prayer meetings are being held on this day, and for that I am deeply grateful. We are a nation under God, and I believe God intended for us to be free. It would be fitting and good, I think, if on each Inauguration Day in future years, it should be declared a day of prayer.

*First inaugural address*
*January 20, 1981*

In one of the conflicts that was going on throughout the past year when views were held deeply on both sides of the debate,

I recall talking to one senator who came into my office. We both deeply believed what it was we were espousing, but we were on opposite sides. And when we finished talking, as he rose, he said, "I'm going out of here and do some praying." And I said, "Well, if you get a busy signal, it's me there ahead of you."

*Annual National Prayer Breakfast*
*Washington, D.C., February 4, 1982*

Today our nation is at peace and is enjoying prosperity; but our need for prayer is even greater. We can give thanks to God for the ever increasing abundance He has bestowed on us, and we can remember all those in our society who are in need of help, whether it be material assistance in the form of charity or simply a friendly word of encouragement. We are all God's handiwork, and it is appropriate for us as individuals and as a nation to call on Him in prayer.

*National Day of Prayer Proclamation*
*January 29, 1985*

# *T*HE PRESIDENCY

Dad in the Oval Office in 1982

*Shortly before Colleen and I were married in late 1975, Dad and Nancy called a family conference at their house in Pacific Palisades. They specifically asked me to bring Colleen, since she was about to become a member of the family.* Hmm, *I thought,* this sounds serious!

*The night of the meeting, Colleen and I picked up my sister, Maureen, and we drove to the house together. As we talked along the way, we were all pretty sure we knew what the family powwow was all about: Dad was going to tell us he had decided to run for president.*

*Ronald Reagan had served eight enormously successful years as governor of California. Meanwhile, the Republican incumbent, Gerald Ford, was considered a goner in the upcoming election, having shot himself in the foot by pardoning his predecessor, Richard Nixon, for Watergate crimes. All of us in the Reagan family knew that Dad—ever the patriotic Boy Scout—believed his party and his country needed him. (Dad was right, even though it would turn out that 1976 wasn't his year to win the White House.)*

*We arrived at Dad and Nancy's house and gathered in the living room for the family meeting. Ron, Maureen, Colleen, and I all sat on a large couch, while Dad and Nancy sat in two chairs facing us. At seventeen, Ron was still living at home, while Patti, who was studying at USC at the time, was not able to come to the family conference that night.*

*With Nancy looking on, Dad began by recounting the fact that he had spent the months since leaving Sacramento doing the kind of work he enjoyed most: traveling around the country, speaking to various groups about his vision for America and how it could be achieved. Then he proceeded to tell us exactly what we expected him to say:*

At every hotel and airport I see "Reagan for President" placards. But you know what really gets to me? Whenever I check into a hotel, the bellmen who carry my bags ask me, "Why don't you run for president? We need you!" Then, as I walk out of my room the next morning, the chambermaids stop me to shake my hand and say the same thing. It doesn't matter where I go, it's always the same. I walk through the airports, and people stop me and say, "Please, we need you to run."

It won't be easy, but the grassroots support is there. I've been speaking out on the issues for quite a while now, and it's time to put myself on the line. In three weeks I'm going to announce I'm entering the race. If I didn't do this, I'd feel like the guy who always sat on the bench and never got into the game.

*October 1975*

*Dad enjoyed the presidency as few in that office have, before or since. To put it in the terms of his previous career, it was the best role he ever had, and he carried it off with more verve, passion, honesty, and authenticity than any other part he played. The role of president suited him, and he dignified, elevated, and honored the presidency more than any of his predecessors since Lincoln.*

*Sure, there were times when his pin-striped suit felt like a straitjacket, and the beautiful ivory walls of the White House closed in on him like a gilded cage. But Dad cheerfully accepted the confinement and restrictions of the office along with the perks and power. From the Oval Office he changed the world. He served the American people well. He preserved, protected, and defended the Constitution of the United States. And when he handed the presidency over to his successor, it was in much better condition than when he received it.*

*Ronald Reagan was a different kind of president than those who came before and after him. He never looked at himself as "the president." Rather, he held the office itself in awe and reverence, and spoke of it as a position he temporarily occupied—and one he wished to honor.*

*Even before he took over the presidency, it became clear to Dad that he had accepted a tough job with a lot of problems. A few days before the inauguration, as he was being briefed on a range of domestic and foreign policy problems, he joked,*

I think I'll demand a recount!

*At the end of his first full day in office, Dad remarked,*

It's been a very wonderful day. I guess I can go back to California—can't I?

*January 21, 1981*

*The next day, in the Oval Office, an aide quoted President Kennedy's assessment of the presidency to him: "The pay is pretty good and you can walk home to lunch." Dad replied,*

Oh? I've been here two days and I've had lunch both days in this office.

*January 22, 1981*

*During his first year in office, he often felt hemmed in by the demands of his busy schedule, prompting him to remark,*

I'm a prisoner of my schedule again.
   *and*
I have no time to be president.

*Because the White House residence is located on the second floor, above the office floor, Dad compared working and living in the White House to the business his father once operated in Tampico, Illinois:*

I'm back living above the store again.

*Here are some of Ronald Reagan's later impressions of the presidency, both humorous and profound.*

One of the great things about being president is that you can invite anyone you want to lunch or dinner, and chances are they'll come.

Speaking My Mind: Selected Speeches
*(New York: Simon & Schuster, 1989), p. 67*

Four years ago I didn't know precisely every duty of this office, and not too long ago, I learned about some new ones from the first-graders of Corpus Christi School in Chambersburg, Pennsylvania. Little Leah Kline was asked by her teacher to describe my duties. She said: "The president goes to meetings. He helps the animals. The president gets frustrated. He talks to other presidents." How does wisdom begin at such an early age?

*Acceptance speech, Republican National Convention*
*Dallas, Texas, August 23, 1984*

One of the things about the presidency is that you're always somewhat apart. You spend a lot of time going by too fast in a car someone else is driving and seeing the people through tinted glass—the parents holding up a child and the wave you saw too late and couldn't return. And so many times I wanted to stop and reach out from behind the glass and connect.

*Farewell address, The Oval Office*
*January 11, 1989*

Nobody asked me what it was going to feel like to not be president anymore. I have some understanding, because after I'd been governor for eight years and then stepped down, I want to tell you what it's like. We'd only been home a few days, and someone invited us out to dinner. Nancy and I both went out, got in the backseat of the car, and waited for somebody to get in front and drive us.

*To Russian students at the end of a question and answer*
*session, Moscow State University, May 31, 1988*

# THE PRESS

It's so . . . frustrating! I'll make a statement, and an hour later, the press or the legislators will say, "Sure, that's what he *says*. But what does he *mean*?" I don't get it. If they could only accept that what I say is what I mean, it would save so much time!

*Said to Nancy Reagan, early in his first term as governor of California*
*Quoted by Nancy Reagan in* My Turn
*(New York: Random House, 1989), p. 111*

But on the level, though, I like photographers. You don't ask questions. Can you imagine [ABC News correspondent] Sam Donaldson with a camera? As most of you would say, "The thought makes me shutter." Somebody asked me one day why we didn't put a stop to Sam's shouting out questions at us when we're out on the South Lawn. We can't. If we did, the starlings would come back.

*Annual awards dinner*
*White House News Photographers Association*
*Washington D.C., May 18, 1983*

1983 was a banner year for America, notwithstanding voices of pessimism, which always found the single dark cloud in every blue sky. Those voices come from many different areas of our society. Recently *The Wall Street Journal* reported on a survey of one of them: the television networks' nightly news coverage of the economy during the last half of 1983. During that entire period, there were four to fifteen economic statistic stories a month, telling us whether inflation, unemployment, interest rates, retail sales, or housing starts were up or down for a given month. The survey found nearly 95 percent of these reports were positive. However, of the 104 lengthy economic news stories in which the networks gave us their interpretation of what was happening, 86 percent were primarily negative. The survey found the economic news in the second half of 1983 was good. But the coverage on network television was still in recession.

Now, please don't get me wrong, every administration must be held accountable. None of us can be excluded from the fury of a free press whenever that's right and proper. But true balance implies consistently showing all faces of America, including hope, optimism, and progress.

*"Economic Recovery," radio address to the nation*
*Camp David, Maryland, March 10, 1984*

One day I saw an article in the paper about a Catholic bishop from Iowa who had led some Nicaraguan refugees out of Nicaragua and across the border into Honduras. The story said they had been attacked by the Contras and rescued by the Sandinistas. Well, I found this disturbing if true, so I tracked him down and called him. He said, yes, he did lead some of his people out, but that the story was exactly backward—they were attacked by the Sandinistas and rescued by the Contras.

On two different occasions I met with Nicaraguan clergymen who'd had their ears cut off with bayonets by the Sandinistas for preaching. I remember one man's story in particular. The Sandinistas had tied this one young Nicaraguan preacher to a tree and cut off his ears. They then cut his throat and ruthlessly said, "Now call upon your God. Maybe He can help you." The clergyman's congregation got to him before he bled to death. He himself told me that story in the Oval Office of the White House. Both ministers were available to the press, and yet their stories never appeared in the major papers or on the evening news.

Speaking My Mind: Selected Speeches
(New York: Simon & Schuster, 1989), p. 146

# $R$ACE RELATIONS

Dad, with Coretta Scott King at his side, signs into law in 1983 the bill making
Martin Luther King Day a national holiday.

*Ronald Reagan was raised with a deep sense of fair play, justice,
and tolerance toward all people, regardless of race—as the following stories and remarks richly attest.*

On one of our out-of-town trips, the [Eureka College football] team had to stay overnight in Dixon; Mac said I had to stay at the hotel with the rest of the team and so I went with him to a downtown hotel to help us register. The hotel manager said, "I can take everybody but your two colored boys."

Mac bristled and said all of us would sleep on the bus that night. Then I suggested another solution: "Mac, why don't you tell those two fellows there isn't enough room in the hotel for everybody so we'll have to break up the team; then put me and them in a cab and send us to my house."

Mac gave me a funny look; he'd just had a chance to observe firsthand what the people of Dixon thought of blacks, and I'm sure he had his doubts my parents would think much of the idea. "You're sure you want to do that?" he asked.

I knew my parents well and said yes. We went to my house and I rang the bell and Nelle came to the door and I told her there wasn't enough room for the whole team at the hotel. "Well, come on in," she said, her eyes brightening with a warmth felt by all three of us.

She was absolutely color blind when it came to racial matters; these fellows were just two of my friends. That was the way she and Jack had always raised my brother and me.

An American Life
*(New York: Simon & Schuster, 1990), p. 52*

★

My parents constantly drummed into me the importance of judging people as *individuals*. There was no more grievous sin at our household than a racial slur or other evidence of religious or racial intolerance. A lot of it, I think, was because my dad had learned what discrimination was like firsthand. He'd grown up in an era when some stores still had signs at their door saying, NO DOGS OR IRISHMEN ALLOWED.

When my brother and I were growing up, there were still ugly tumors of racial bigotry in much of America, including the corner of Illinois where we lived. At our one local movie theater, blacks and whites had to sit apart—the blacks in the balcony. My mother and father urged my brother and me to bring home our black playmates, to consider them equals, and to respect the religious views of our friends, whatever they were. My brother's best friend was black, and when they went to the movies, Neil sat with him in the balcony.

Once my father checked into a hotel during a shoe-selling trip and a clerk told him: "You'll like it here, Mr. Reagan, we don't permit a Jew in the place."

My father, who told us the story later, said he looked at the clerk angrily and picked up his suitcase and left. "I'm a Catholic," he said. "If it's come to the point where you won't take Jews, then some day you won't take *me* either."

Because it was the only hotel in town, he spent the night in his car during a winter blizzard and I think it may have led to his first heart attack.

An American Life
*(New York: Simon & Schuster, 1990), pp. 30–31*

We don't lump people by groups or special interests. And let me add, in the party of Lincoln there is no room for intolerance and not even a small corner for anti-Semitism or bigotry of any kind. Many people are welcome in our house, but not the bigots.

*Acceptance speech, Republican National Convention*
*Dallas, Texas, August 23, 1984*

I was never able to convince many black citizens of my commitment to their needs. They often mistook my belief in keeping the government out of the average American's life as a cover for doing nothing about racial injustice.

I think of all things that were said about me during my presidency, this charge bothers me the most personally. I abhor racism. These skinheads and white supremacist groups have no place in this country. They are not what we are about, and I wish they would just vaporize.

Speaking My Mind: Selected Speeches
*(New York: Simon & Schuster, 1989), pp. 163–164*

# RADIO

Dad as an announcer on WHO Radio in Des Moines, Iowa, in the 1930s

*The common denominator among all of Dad's various careers was radio. He got his start in the entertainment business as a radio sports announcer. During his years as an actor in Hollywood, he was in numerous radio dramas and comedy*

*shows. Even as president he had a regular radio gig—his Saturday radio commentaries. So you might say I'm carrying on the family business with my own syndicated radio show. I'm even heard over the station that gave Dad his start in the broadcasting biz—WHO in Des Moines.*

I've always loved radio. My first job out of college was as a radio sportscaster, and it was one of the happiest times of my life. I had a fun job, a new car, a certain amount of fame and recognition there in the Midwest. I was having a good time. Eventually I got a crack at working in motion pictures, and I left radio, but it always had a certain hold on my heart.

Speaking My Mind: Selected Speeches
*(New York: Simon & Schuster, 1989), p. 51*

I spent four years at station WHO in Des Moines and they were among the most pleasant of my life. At twenty-two I'd achieved my dream: I was a sports announcer. If I had stopped there, I believe I would have been happy the rest of my life.

An American Life
*(New York: Simon & Schuster, 1990), p. 71*

# RELIGIOUS FREEDOM

Freedom prospers when religion is vibrant and the rule of law under God is acknowledged. When our Founding Fathers passed the First Amendment, they sought to protect churches from government interference. They never intended to construct a wall of hostility between government and the concept of religious belief itself.

*Annual convention of the*
*National Association of Evangelicals*
*Orlando, Florida, March 8, 1983*

A state is nothing more than a reflection of its citizens; the more decent the citizens, the more decent the state. If you practice a religion, whether you're Catholic, Protestant, Jewish, or guided by some other faith, then your private life will be influenced by a sense of moral obligation, and so, too, will your public life. One affects the other. The churches of America do not exist by the grace of the state; the churches of America are not mere citizens of the state. The churches of America exist apart; they have their own vantage point; their own authority. Religion is its own realm; it makes its own claims.

We establish no religion in this country, nor will we ever. We command no worship. We mandate no belief. But we poison our society when we remove its theological underpinnings. We court corruption when we leave it bereft of belief. All are free to believe or not believe; all are free to practice a faith or not. But those who believe must be free to speak of and act on their belief, to apply moral teaching to public questions.

*Address before the Ecumenical Prayer Breakfast*
*Republican National Convention*
*Dallas, Texas, August 23, 1984*

# REPUBLICAN PARTY

So it was our Republican party that gave me a political home. When I signed up for duty, I didn't have to check my principles at the door. And I soon found out that the desire for victory did not overcome our devotion to ideals.

*Republican National Convention*
*New Orleans, Louisiana, August 15, 1988*

I refuse to believe that the good Lord divided this world into Republicans who defend basic values and Democrats who win elections.

*"Reshaping the American Political Landscape"*
*American Conservative Union Banquet*
*Washington, D.C., February 6, 1977*

We do have a rendezvous with destiny. Either we will preside over the great nightfall for all mankind, or we will accept the leadership that has been thrust upon us. I believe that is the obligation and responsibility of the Republican party today.

*"Why the Conservative Movement Is Growing"*
*Southern GOP Convention*
*Atlanta, Georgia, December 7, 1973*

★

I believe the Republican party can and should provide the political mechanism through which the goals of the majority of Americans can be achieved. For one thing, the biggest single grouping of conservatives is to be found in that party. It makes more sense to build on that grouping than to break it up and start over. Rather than a third party, we can have a new first party made up of people who share our principles. I have said before that if a formal change in name proves desirable, then so be it. But tonight, for purpose of discussion, I'm going to refer to it simply as the New Republican party.

And let me say this so there can be no mistake as to what I mean: the New Republican party I envision will not, and cannot, be one limited to the country club big business image that, for reasons, both fair and unfair, it is burdened with today. The New Republican party I am speaking about is going to have room for the man and woman in the factories, for the farmer, for the cop on the beat, and the millions of Americans who may never have thought of joining our party before but whose interests coincide with those represented by principled Republicanism.

If we are to attract more working men and women of this country, we will do so not simply by "making room" for them, but by making certain they have a say in what goes on in the party. The Democratic party turned its back on the majority of social conservatives during the 1960s. The New Republican party of the late '70s and '80s must welcome them, seek them out, enlist them, not only as rank-and-file members but as leaders and as candidates.

*"Reshaping the American Political Landscape"*
*American Conservative Union Banquet*
*Washington, D.C., February 6, 1977*

# RIGHT TO LIFE

I think all of us should have a respect for innocent life. With regard to the freedom of the individual for choice with regard to abortion, there's one individual who's not being considered at all. That's the one who is being aborted. And I've noticed that everybody who is for abortion has already been born. I think that, technically—I know this is a difficult and an emotional problem, and many people sincerely feel on both sides of this—but I do believe that maybe we could find the answer through medical evidence, if we would determine once and for all: Is an unborn child a human being? I happen to believe it is.

*The Reagan–Carter Debate, October 28, 1980*

I, too, have always believed that God's greatest gift is human life and that we have a duty to protect the life of an unborn child. Until someone can prove the unborn child is not a life, shouldn't we give it the benefit of the doubt and assume it is?

*"Domestic Social Issues," radio address to the nation*
*Camp David, Maryland, January 22, 1983*

A Supreme Court decision literally wiped off the books of fifty states statutes protecting the rights of unborn children. Abortion on demand now takes the lives of up to one and a half million unborn children a year. Human life legislation ending this tragedy will someday pass the Congress, and you and I must never rest until it does.

*Annual convention of the*
*National Association of Evangelicals*
*Orlando, Florida, March 8, 1983*

# SCHOOL PRAYER

We are told that God is dead. Well, He isn't. We just can't talk to Him in the classroom anymore.

*California, 1966*

Where were we when God was expelled from the classroom?

*Eisenhower College fund-raiser speech, October 14, 1969*

I believe that schoolchildren deserve the same right to pray that's enjoyed by the Congress and chaplains and troops in our armed services. The motto on our coinage reads, "In God We Trust." No one must ever be forced or pressured to take part in any religious exercise, but neither should the government forbid religious practice. The public expression through prayer of our faith in God is a fundamental part of our American heritage and a privilege which should not be excluded from our schools.

*"Domestic Social Issues," radio address to the nation*
*Camp David, Maryland, January 22, 1983*

# SCHOOL PRAYER

I know that some believe that voluntary prayer in schools should be restricted to a moment of silence. We already have the right to remain silent—we can take our Fifth Amendment.

*National Religious Broadcasters annual convention*
*January 30, 1984*

From the early days of the colonies, prayer in school was practiced and revered as an important tradition. Indeed, for nearly two hundred years of our nation's history, it was considered a natural expression of our religious freedom. But in 1962 the Supreme Court handed down a controversial decision prohibiting prayer in public schools.

Sometimes I can't help but feel the First Amendment is being turned on its head. Because, ask yourselves: Can it really be true that the First Amendment can permit Nazis and Ku Klux Klansmen to march on public property, advocate the extermination of people of the Jewish faith and the subjugation of blacks, while the same amendment forbids our children from saying a prayer in school?

*"Prayer in Public Schools," radio address to the nation*
*Camp David, Maryland, February 25, 1984*

Dad and Gorbachev in Moscow's Red Square in 1988

# THE SOVIET UNION

*Today, the Soviet Union is a memory. We easily forget how the world was in the 1980s when Ronald Reagan boldly consigned the Soviet system to "the ash heap of history." On Inauguration Day 1981, it looked as if America was headed for the ash heap.*

*It took a man of rare courage and vision to see that the potential existed to completely alter the course of history, to "begin the world over again" (as Thomas Paine once put it). It took a man of rare conviction to decide that the time had come to end the stalemate between the superpowers and liberate half of the globe from totalitarian oppression.*

*That man, of course, was my father, Ronald Reagan.*

It is the Soviet Union that runs against the tide of history . . . [It is] the march of freedom and democracy which will leave Marxism–Leninism on the ash heap of history, as it has left other tyrannies which stifle the freedom and muzzle the self-expression of the people.

*Address to members of the British Parliament,*
*Palace of Westminster, June 8, 1982*

If the Soviet Union let another political party come into existence, they would still be a one-party state, because everybody would join the other party.

*June 23, 1983*

I have openly expressed my view of the Soviet system. I don't know why this should come as a surprise to Soviet leaders, who have never shied from expressing their view of our system. But this doesn't mean that we can't deal with each other. We don't refuse to talk when the Soviets call us imperialist aggressors and worse, or because they cling to the fantasy of a Communist triumph over democracy. The fact that neither of us likes the other system is no reason to refuse to talk.

*Address to the nation on U.S.–Soviet relations*
*January 16, 1984*

It's no secret that I wear a hearing aid. Well, just the other day, all of a sudden, it went haywire. We discovered the KGB had put a listening device in my listening device.

*White House Correspondents Association annual dinner*
*Washington, D.C., April 22, 1987*

I am a collector of stories that I can establish are actually told by the people of the Soviet Union among themselves. And this one has to do with the fact that in the Soviet Union, if you want to buy an automobile, there is a ten-year wait. And you have to put the money down ten years before you get the car.

So, there was a young fellow there that had finally made it, and he was going through all the bureaus and agencies that he had to go through and signing all the papers, and finally got to the last agency where they put the stamp on it. And then he gave them his money, and they said, "Come back in ten years and get your car."

And he said, "Morning or afternoon?"

And the man that had put the stamp on said, "Well, wait a minute, we're talking about ten years from now. What difference does it make?"

He said, "The plumber is coming in the morning."

*Reception for Senator Orrin Hatch*
*June 17, 1987*

# Taxes

*As president, Ronald Reagan understood the powerful, negative impact taxes have on the American family. He knew that time spent working at extra jobs to pay taxes is time spent away from the family, time robbed from children, time that can never be repaid once a child has outgrown the formative years. The crushing tax burden inflicted on us by our government forces parents to work two or three jobs and literally translates to children who are not read to, talked to, listened to, prayed with, hugged, or cuddled as much as they need. According to the nonpartisan Tax Foundation, the average American family now spends more on taxes than on shelter, food, clothing, and transportation combined.*

Confiscatory taxes bear a Democratic trademark. Since the inception of the federal income tax in 1914, it has been increased thirteen times under Democratic administrations. It has been reduced eight times under Republican administrations.

*"Why the Conservative Movement Is Growing"*
*Southern GOP Convention, Atlanta, Georgia, December 7, 1973*

I've been told that some members of Congress disagree with my tax cut proposal. Well, you know it's been said that taxation is the art of plucking the feathers without killing the bird. It's time they realized the bird just doesn't have any feathers left.

*Mid-Winter Congressional City Conference*
*of the National League of Cities, March 2, 1981*

Like federal employees, taxpayers also work for the government—they just don't have to take a civil service exam. Here in America, land of opportunity, governments at all levels are taxing away 40 percent of our nation's income. We've been creeping closer to socialism, a system that someone once said works only in heaven, where it isn't needed, and in hell, where they've already got it.

*"Federal Income Taxation," radio address to the nation*
*Camp David, Maryland, April 9, 1983*

Tax rates are prices—prices for working, saving, and investing. And when you raise the price of those productive activities, you get less of them and more activity in the underground economy, tax shelters, and leisure pursuits. You in small business understand that you can't force people to buy merchandise that isn't selling by raising your price. But too many in Washington and across the country still believe that we can raise more revenue from the economy by making it more expensive to work, save, and invest in the economy. We can't repeal human nature.

*National Federation of Independent Business conference*
*Washington, D.C., June 22, 1983*

And what about fairness for families? It's in our families that America's most important work gets done—raising our next generation. But over the last forty years, as inflation has shrunk the personal exemption, families with children have had to shoulder more and more of the tax burden. With inflation and bracket-creep also eroding incomes, many spouses who would rather stay home with their children have been forced to go looking for jobs.

*Signing the Tax Reform Act of 1986*
*White House South Lawn October 22, 1986*

No nation in history has ever survived a tax burden that reached a third of its national income.

*"A Time for Choosing" (a.k.a. "The Speech")*
*Televised address to the nation on behalf of*
*Barry Goldwater, October 27, 1964*

In 1980 the people decided with us that the economic crisis was not caused by the fact that they lived too well. Government lived too well. It was time for tax increases to be an act of last resort, not of first resort. The people told the liberal leadership in Washington, "Try shrinking the size of government before you shrink the size of our paychecks."

*Acceptance speech, Republican National Convention*
*Dallas, Texas, August 23, 1984*

England may be the mother of parliaments, but from the Boston Tea Party to this administration, it's the United States that has been the mother of tax revolts.

You know, that's a pretty good line. I can hardly wait to try it out on Margaret Thatcher.

*Briefing for the American Business Conference*
*The White House, March 23, 1988*

Republicans believe every day is the Fourth of July, but Democrats believe every day is April 15.

*Said on several occasions*

# *T*RUTH

I'm not smart enough to lie.

*July 1980*

Anyone who seeks success or greatness should first forget about both and seek only the truth. The rest will follow.

*Conservative Political Action Conference*
*Washington, D.C., March 20, 1981*

In the face of a climate of falsehood and misinformation, we've promised the world a season of truth—the truth of our great civilized ideas: individual liberty, representative government, the rule of law under God.

*First State of the Union address*
*January 26, 1982*

# $V$ALUES

What do we want for ourselves and our children? Is it enough to have material things? Aren't liberty and morality and integrity and high principles and a sense of responsibility more important? The world's truly great thinkers have not pointed us toward materialism; they have dealt with the great truths and with the high questions of right and wrong, of morality and of integrity.

*"The Value of Understanding the Past"*
*Eureka College Library Dedication*
*September 28, 1967*

We didn't discover our values in a poll taken a week before the convention.

*Acceptance speech, Republican National Convention*
*Dallas, Texas, August 23, 1984*

[Our goal] is to help revive America's traditional values: faith, family, neighborhood, work, and freedom. Government has no business enforcing these values but neither must it seek, as it did in the recent past, to suppress or replace them. That only robbed us of our tiller and set us adrift.

Helping to restore these values will bring new strength, direction, and dignity to our lives and to the life of our nation. It's on these values that we'll best build our future.

*"Goals for the Future," radio address to the nation*
*Camp David, Maryland, August 25, 1984*

Loyalty, faithfulness, commitment, courage, patriotism, the ability to distinguish between right and wrong—I hope that these values are as much a part of your life as any calculus course or social science study. And so, do remember: Gratitude is a way to a deeper wisdom. Look for that deeper wisdom. Believe me, there's a great hunger for it. And here you're in luck. As Americans, you have a special claim on it.

*Presentation ceremony, Presidential Scholars Awards*
*Washington, D.C., June 16, 1988*

# VETERANS

*Ronald Reagan was governor of California during the height of the Vietnam War, and he and Nancy became very involved in the plight of the American prisoners of that war. Dad and Nancy visited, phoned, and corresponded with many of the families of the POWs. At the end of the war they watched along with millions of others as the first flight of POWs touched down on American soil. Later they opened their home and held a series of dinner receptions for the men who were coming home to California.*

It's not been too many months, not quite a year, that we sat up until the late hours and watched on television when that first plane came into Clark Field. We saw those men when the plane door opened. We didn't know what we were going to see. Would they be zombies, would they be robots, as the result of seven, eight, nine years of torture and confinement? And then that first American came down the ramp, saluted the flag, and said: "God bless America."

Nancy and I have had an experience. About a hundred-fifty of

Dad in his U.S. Army Air Force uniform in the 1940s

those returning prisoners of war were from California. We had them, and some who weren't from California, as guests in our home, just after their return. It was an unforgettable experience.

We saw men come into our home, who for nine years had been the most intimate of buddies in prison camps. And suddenly they looked at each other, and we heard them acknowledge this was the first time they had ever seen each other face to face. Their intimate friendship had been built up through bamboo walls, tapping on the walls, with the code and the signals that they had invented. They told us of the things they did to harass the enemy with their code.

There were other stories. They told us of men that had been tortured, lying on the other side of the wall in the next cell near death. And all they could do was lie on their side of the cell, hour after hour, taking turns all night long, tapping on the wall, just to tell them they were not alone, to keep in there, to hang on.

Some said, "You know, we thought you'd throw rocks at us when we came home." They didn't feel they could serve any longer. They were imprisoned. So they resisted torture as long as they could, but they said eventually the enemy got what he wanted.

Someone, one night in our home, said to them, "Well, if you knew you were going to have to talk and give in, why didn't you do that first? Why did you take that torture?"

And they looked with astonishment and said, "Holding out was the only thing left for us to do; the only thing we could still do for our country."

Later I asked Nancy, "Where do we find men like this?" And almost as quickly as I asked the question, I knew the answer. We find them on the farms, in small towns, in the city streets of America—just ordinary guys named Joe, produced by this society of ours.

*"Why the Conservative Movement Is Growing"*
*Southern GOP Convention*
*Atlanta, Georgia, December 7, 1973*

That fellow with the thickening waist and the thinning hair who is sometimes unreasonable about your allowance or letting you have the car—his life seems a little dull to you now as he reports for his daily nine-to-five chores, or looks forward to lowering a golf handicap, or catching a fish no one wants to eat.

I wish you could have known him a few years back on a landing craft at Normandy or Tarawa or on a weekend pass in Peoria. He was quite a guy. Winston Churchill said he was the only man in the world who could laugh and fight at the same time. General Marshall called him our secret weapon. He hated war more than he hated the enemy, but he did what had to be done.

*"The Value of Understanding the Past"*
*Eureka College Library Dedication*
*September 28, 1967*

# WELFARE STATE

The doctor's fight against socialized medicine is your fight. We can't socialize the doctors without socializing the patients.

*"A Time for Choosing" (a.k.a. "The Speech")*
*Televised address to the nation on behalf of*
*Barry Goldwater, October 27, 1964*

You and I are told we must choose between a left or right, but I suggest there is no such thing as a left or right. There is only an up or down. Up to man's age-old dream—the maximum of individual freedom consistent with order—or down to the ant heap of totalitarianism. Regardless of their sincerity, their humanitarian motives, those who would sacrifice freedom for security have embarked on this downward path. Plutarch warned, "The real destroyer of the liberties of the people is he who spreads among them bounties, donations, and benefits."

*"A Time for Choosing" (a.k.a. "The Speech")*
*Televised address to the nation on behalf of*
*Barry Goldwater, October 27, 1964*

We learned, of course, that there are people who'll cheat, and there are those who'll accept a lower standard of living in order to get by without working. But we also learned that the overwhelming majority of welfare recipients would like nothing better than to be self-supporting, with a job and a place in our productive society. They may be fed and sheltered by welfare, but as human beings, they are being destroyed by it.

There is a giant bureaucratic complex that thinks of them as "clients," to be permanently maintained as government dependents. This complex measures its own well being and success by how much the welfare rolls increase. To be truly successful, the goal should be to reduce the rolls by eliminating the need for welfare. This is the kind of common sense that's been lacking in Washington for much too long.

*"Government and the Family: The Need to Restore Basic Values"*
*Televised address to the nation, July 6, 1976*

America is a wealthy nation, but our wealth is not unlimited. So we've tried to face up to the reality too many have ignored. Unless we prune nonessential programs, unless we end benefits for those who should not be subsidized by their fellow taxpayers, we won't have enough resources to meet the requirements of those who must have our help. And helping those who truly need assistance is what fairness in government spending should be all about.

*"Economic and Fair Housing Issues,"*
*radio address to the nation*
*Camp David, Maryland, July 9, 1983*

I think the best possible social program is a job.

*Trevose, Pennsylvania, 1980*

We don't celebrate dependence day on the Fourth of July. We celebrate Independence Day.

*Acceptance speech, Republican National Convention*
*Dallas, Texas, August 23, 1984*

Nations crumble from within when the citizenry asks of government those things which the citizenry might better provide for itself.

*April 7, 1975*

# AFTERWORD

## My Uncommon Father, Ronald Reagan

Ronald Reagan casts a long shadow. His footprints are great and his stride is long. The Gipper is a tough act to follow.

But follow it we must. Because the job Ronald Reagan set out to do is not yet finished.

Dad closes his autobiography, *An American Life,* with the story of his journey home to California at the conclusion of his presidency. It was his last flight aboard Air Force One. Shortly before the plane landed, Dad and Nancy, along with the staff, press, and Secret Service who were aboard, embraced one another and posed for pictures. Bottles of champagne were popped open and glasses were raised. Someone called out, "Mission accomplished, Mr. President!"

"Not yet, I thought to myself, not yet," writes Ronald Reagan. And there his book ends.

Dad was right. The Reagan presidency is not finished. The Reagan mission is not yet accomplished. The Reagan legacy has not yet been probated. The City on a Hill that Ronald Reagan envisioned throughout his public life has not yet been built. In fact, we have neglected and retreated from the blueprint he left us.

My hope, in collecting these words of Ronald Reagan—words culled from both private conversations and public pronouncements, from the 1950s through the 1990s—is that you and I would recapture the spark, the inspiration, the passion, and the dream of Ronald Reagan. It's up to you and me to complete what he began. Dad has been sidelined, but you and I are still in the game, and it's up to us to get in there and win one for the Gipper.

You may think, "Well, who am I? Just one person—one common, ordinary person." But the secret of Ronald Reagan's success was that he, too, was a common, everyday person—but with an uncommon love for America and an uncommon commitment to leaving this nation a better place than he found it.

He believed that a free America could unleash the engine of prosperity, and the economy would roar back to life. He believed that a strong America could face down the Soviet bear and defeat Communist totalitarianism without firing a shot. He believed that a courageous and morally upright America could demand that the Berlin Wall be torn down, and it would fall. And he was right on all counts.

The sun has set on Ronald Reagan's life. But for the rest of us it is still high noon. We have a job to do, and we'd better get to it. We have a lot of praying, phoning, faxing, E-mailing, contributing, volunteering, and campaigning to do—so what are we waiting for? Remember, there are three kinds of people in this world: those who make it happen, those who watch it happen, and those who wonder what happened. It's up to you and me to make things happen.

I've shared with you the words of the greatest man I've ever known, a man I am privileged to call my father. So read his words, then heed his words.

Join me, will you? There's plenty of work to do. Come on! Let's go out and win one more for the Gipper!

Dad says good-bye on his last day in office on January 20, 1989.

# LOOK FOR THESE OTHER BOOKS BY MICHAEL REAGAN

### The City on a Hill

Michael Reagan, son of former president Ronald Reagan, draws on his father's own words, plus fascinating stories from his life to present a blueprint for rebuilding the "city on a hill" and his father's vision for America in the next millennium.

**0-7852-7236-4 • Hardcover • 288 pages**

### Making Waves

As the son of Ronald Reagan and actress Jane Wyman, Michael Reagan grew up in the public eye. But his relentless, outspoken conservatism, passion, and knife-edged wit is what has made him the most popular night-time radio talk show host in the nation. In this book, he allows readers a glimpse of his life, his values, and his vision for America.

**0-7852-7588-6 • Hardcover • 304 pages**
**Also available in audio 0-7852-7219-4 •**
**Approximately 120 minutes**

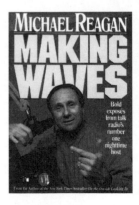